Prayer and Revival

Prayer and Revival
Copyright ©1975; 2003 by Midnight Call Ministries
Published by The Olive Press a subsidiary of Midnight Call Inc.
Columbia, South Carolina, 29228

Copy Editor: Susanna Cancassi
Proofreaders: Angie Peters, Susanna Cancassi
Layout/Design: Michelle Kim
Lithography: Simon Froese
Cover Design: Michelle Kim

Library of Congress Cataloging-in-Publication Data

Malgo, Wim

Prayer and Revival
ISBN #0-937422-12-6

1. Biblical Teaching   3. Prophecy
2. Counselling

Printed in the United States of America

Contents

❧

Foreword By Arno Froese   **11**

Introduction   **13**

Chapter 1   **15**

The Divine Conditions For Revival

Revival Or Judgment? • The Sins Of The Eyes • The Sins Of The Heart • The Sins Of The Tongue • What Are The Divine Conditions For Revival?

Chapter 2   **29**

Pathway To Revival

A Prophetic Widow • The Great Debt • God's Children In Bondage

Chapter 3   43

How Does Revival Begin?

There's No Turning Back! • The Battle Is Against The Root
Of All Evil • Get Back To The Bible!

Chapter 4   57

Does God Want To Send A Revival?

What Is God's Will? • His Will Is Our Sanctification • Two
Ways • Water And Fire • Endtimes Fire • The Need For Revival
• Revival Is Not A Miracle • Break Up The Fallow Ground •
Revival Will Lead To Israel • Judgment In The Church

Chapter 5   75

What Is Our Calling?

Holy Spirit Leadership • The Lord Is The Spirit • God Never
Repeats Himself

Chapter 6   81

Seven Aspects Of Prayer

Are We Ready To Receive? • Are We Ready For The Whole
Truth? • Are We Ready To Believe? • Are We Ready To Have
Our Souls Searched? • Are We Ready To Be Reconciled? • Are
We Ready To Take? • Are We Ready For A Completely New,
Worldwide And Glorious Commission?

Chapter 7   89

How To Prepare For Victorious Prayer

The Key • Ye Ask And Receive Not • Resist The Devil • Go
Through The Gates • Break Up Your Fallow Ground

Chapter 8   99

Conditions For Answers To Prayer

We Must Take Time • Seek Your Place • Listen Before
You Speak

Chapter 9   107

What The Lord Wants To See

A Perfect Heart • A Contrite Spirit • Trembling At His Word
• In Great Affliction

Chapter 10   115

Prayer In Times Of Trouble

Humiliating Trials • Calling Upon The Lord of Lords •
Mary • Jabez • The Enemy Of Faith • Build The Altar •
Fervent Prayer

Chapter 11   123

What Does It Mean To "Break Through" In Prayer?

Unconfessed Sin • Family Tradition • Job • Daniel • Korah •
David • Jesus

Chapter 12   131

When God Is Silenced

When God Doesn't Answer • An Interrupted Relationship
With The Lord • Interrupted By Sin

Chapter 13   137

Resistance Against Prayer

Resistance From The Invisible World • Resistance From The
Visible World • Resistance Of Prayer Within Us • Laziness •
The Loss Of Our First Love

Chapter 14   145

Prayer In The Name Of Jesus

In Jesus' Name • Walk As He Walked • Follow His Way • The
Way Of The Lamb • The Way Of Humility • The Goal Is The
Father • Glorify God

Chapter 15   153

Prayer Out Of A Knowledge Of God

Abiding In Jesus • Christ Lives In Us By Faith • We Are In
Heaven • He Is Our Father • We Must Know The Father •
Perfect In Him • The Father's Eternal Faithfulness • Little
Children • Young Children • Young Men • Fathers • Prayer
Warriors • Abraham • Elijah • Paul

Chapter 16   165

The Importance Of Giving Thanks

Jehoshaphat • Offering Thanks Glorifies God • Victorious
Thanksgiving • Priestly Thanksgiving • Unpleasant
Thanksgiving

Chapter 17   173

The Restored Altar

Moses' Altar • Noah's Altar • Abraham's Altar • An Altar In
The Name Of The Lord • The Restored Altar • Broken
Sacrifice • Evening Sacrifice • Your Decision

Chapter 18   185

Three Stages Of Revival

Personal Revival • Spreading Of Revival • General Revival

Chapter 19   191

Revival Among God's People

Where Does Revival Begin? • He Was Obedient To The Lord
• He Had An Open Sanctuary • He Repaired The Doors • He
Re-Enlisted The Priests And Levites • He Gathered Them •
He Revealed The Damage • He Renewed The Covenant With
The Lord • They Trespassed • They Turned Their Backs •
They Shut The Doors • The Light Went Out • No Incense
Offered • No Burnt Offerings

Chapter 20   203

The Last Preparation For Revival

The Great Challenge • The Beginning Of Revival • The
Sacrificial Lamb

Chapter 21   211

A Solemn Call For Revival

Keep Silent! • Are You Ready For Revival? • Renew Your
Strength • The Waters Of Blessings • Come Near • Now
Speak

Foreword

❧

"Elias was a man subject to like passions as we are, and he prayed earnestly that it might not rain: and it rained not on the earth by the space of three years and six months"(James 5:17).

The simplicity of the above Scripture is overwhelming: Elijah prayed and God acted. How could he have been so sure God would answer? Because he lived in the presence of the Lord; therefore, he had full assurance that he was doing His will.

Dr. Wim Malgo went home to be with the Lord on August 8, 1992. He was a believer just like you and I, but one distinction set him apart: he was a man of prayer. When he began Midnight Call Ministry in 1955, he built the ministry on prayer. His prayers were unusual, unique and directed to heaven. I never heard him repeat phrases in his prayers; they were always new, fresh and offered in child-like faith. It doesn't surprise me that Midnight Call Ministry has experienced such phenomenal growth. No decision about the ministry has ever been made that hasn't first been brought to the Lord in prayer.

The book you are about to read is a collection of the heart-stirring messages Dr. Malgo presented during many of his crusades. You will quickly be able to identify the motive behind Wim Malgo's speaking and writing: to lead the reader or listener closer to the Lord. May the Lord pour a spirit of prayer upon His believing children in these endtimes. Revival will take place in our lives, our families, the Church and the world when we pray honestly and with complete dedication.

Arno Froese, Director
Midnight Call Ministries
October 2002

Introduction

੨●

The content of this book is based upon the promises outlined in God's Word regarding His willingness to send revival. God's grace has allowed us to witness the joy of seeing and experiencing the fulfillment of His divine promises. Nevertheless, we have purposely refrained from writing about personal revival experiences or revivals in the form of crusades or conferences. While these accounts may be beneficial and encouraging to believers, they are, nonetheless, subjective. Our God is almighty. He does great things because of His infinite versatility. He never repeats Himself! Therefore, although personal accounts of revival may be inspiring, heartwarming and refreshing, I firmly believe that the content of God's Word carries immeasurably more weight. When we rely solely on the Word of God and persevere in prayer for revival on the grounds of His Word, we avoid the danger of imitation. God wants to reveal Himself to us in an absolutely new, glorious and unique way. It is our sincere prayer to God, of whom Jesus said, "…is not the God of the dead, but the God of the living," that through these simple expositions, many hearts will be drawn to the Lord so that His Name will be praised through revival in these endtimes.

–Wim Malgo
April 1975

Chapter 1

The Divine Conditions For Revival

What is revival? Revival is nothing other than the working of the triune God. Jesus said that He is not the God of the dead, but of the living.

୨●

God the Father creates life. God the Son also creates life. We see this from the cry: "The Lord is risen indeed!" Jesus Christ brought about an eternally valid revival through His substitutional death on Calvary's Cross followed by His Resurrection. He said: "I live and ye shall live also." This applies in the truest sense of the word.

God the Holy Spirit also creates life. He is the Spirit of revival. At Pentecost, the Holy Spirit visibly descended upon the disciples and caused a revival. At this we can only cry: "O, breath of life come sweeping through us. Revive Thy Church with life and power."

From Ezekiel 37 we see that it is the Holy Spirit's task to work revival. As the dry bones of Israel came together and were covered with flesh, there came a wind (Spirit) from above and it resulted in life.

The triune God already produced revival at the creation of the world. The Living God spoke in the plural form in Genesis 1:26 when He said: "Let us...." And then it says: "And God created." That is the Father spoken of in verse 27. Furthermore, it says: "And God said" (verse 29 and eight more times in the first chapter). That is the Son, for He is the WORD from the beginning. "And the Spirit of God moved upon the face of the waters" (verse 2) testifies to the working of the Holy Spirit as the third person of the Trinity at creation. Creation was revival. We all know the result: light, life, warmth, fruit. All of God's works are life and revival. According to Ephesians 7:10, those who profess to be born again are His workmanship; therefore, we are destined to live. The conclusion of these basic yet monumental facts that confront us today are as follows:

1) **Where there is no revival, we no longer see the Lord at work; we see ourselves at work.** We can do a lot, even in the religious realm, but no life breaks

16

through when we, not God, are at work. Then, as Hebrews 9:14 says, we produce dead works. How necessary is it to be convinced that the words of the Lord in John 15:5 still apply? We can do nothing without Him! If true fellowship with Him is absent, our work is in vain. We already mentioned a sure sign of this: Where there is no revival, the Lord is no longer at work. We are merely carrying out religious activities, and our work is powerless.

Without revival, we are like Samson, who rose up against his enemies. These shattering words about him are found in Judges 16:20: "And he wist not that the LORD was departed from him." This is terrible. When we toil and strive in the Lord's work, without the Lord Himself being at work, everything we do becomes empty and pointless.

Moses realized this and refused to go any further without the Lord. He knew that life in that arid desert only existed when the Lord was with them. He cried: "If thy presence go not with me, carry us not up hence" (Exodus 33:15).

2) **There is death where there is no revival.** The exalted Lord accused the Church of this in Revelation 3:1: "I know thy works, that thou hast a name that thou livest, and art dead." This describes a Christian religion without a living substance. It is useless. A Church without revival becomes detached from the Lord and exists without content or direction.

3) **There is no truth where there is no revival.** The Lord warned of this apostasy: "Why do ye not under-

stand my speech? even because ye cannot hear my word. Ye are of your father the devil, and the lusts of your father ye will do. He was a murderer from the beginning, and abode not in the truth, because there is no truth in him. When he speaketh a lie, he speaketh of his own: for he is a liar, and the father of it" (John 8:43–44). Lies are a part of Satan's character. Few believers abide in and love the truth to the end. It is very significant that the Lord said: "…When he speaketh a lie, he speaketh of his own…," because the self-centered believer always lies. Even if he speaks of the Lord, he is actually seeking his own.

So, then, who needs to be revived? Not the lost; they need to be saved. Children of God who were once alive need to be revived. Revival must begin in the heart of the believer.

The Lord lamented in Isaiah 1:2–3: "Hear, O heavens, and give ear, O earth: for the LORD hath spoken, I have nourished and brought up children, and they have rebelled against me. The ox knoweth his owner, and the ass his master's crib: but Israel doth not know, my people doth not consider." It is as if the Lord were saying: "I have children who are born again, but they believe, live, pray and sing without Me. I have brought them up, I have blessed them and kept them, but they have departed from Me; they have fallen away from Me."

Revival Or Judgment?

We are not concerned with outward apostasy, but

with inner apostasy. The Lord wept in Jeremiah 15:6: "Thou hast forsaken me, saith the LORD, thou art gone backward: therefore will I stretch out my hand against thee, and destroy thee; I am weary with repenting." Today the entire world faces a choice: revival or judgment.

Isaiah 40:28 said that the eternal God does not faint, nor is He weary, yet He lamented in this verse: "I am weary with repenting." God becomes weary when He can no longer work or send revival because of the stubborn disobedience found in His children. We are in the midst of the apostasy and everything is racing ahead in religious activity, but the people do not know that the Lord has departed from them.

How is God's weariness expressed? "Why should ye be stricken any more? ye will revolt more and more" (Isaiah 1:5). In the Christian world, much energy, time and money are wasted in things the Lord does not accept. This is proven in Isaiah 1:13–14: "Bring no more vain oblations; incense is an abomination unto me; the new moons and sabbaths, the calling of assemblies, I cannot away with; it is iniquity, even the solemn meeting. Your new moons and your appointed feasts my soul hateth: they are a trouble unto me; I am weary to bear them." Through Amos, the Lord said: "I hate, I despise your feast days, and I will not smell in your solemn assemblies" (Amos 5:21). Verse 23 of the same chapter says: "Take thou away from me the noise of thy songs; for I will not hear the melody of thy viols."

Clearly, the Lord explains that there are such things as pointless festivals, fruitless Christian meetings and futile singing of choirs. The Lord closes His ears to events such as these when they lack participants' obedience and faith. When He cannot add His "Amen" to these things, He cannot send revival. Remember, those who need to be revived were once alive. How is it possible for believers who were once alive and who lived for the Lord to need revival? Sin. Three particular sins hinder and interrupt revival; they are: 1) the sins of the eyes; 2) the sins of the heart; and 3) the sins of the tongue. Let's take a brief look at each of them.

The Sins Of The Eyes

David serves as a good example of a man extraordinarily blessed by God. We may even call him the "king of a revival." However, the revival he experienced was extinguished because of the sin of the lust of the eyes: "And it came to pass in an eveningtide, that David arose from off his bed, and walked upon the roof of the king's house: and from the roof he SAW a woman washing herself; and the woman was very beautiful to look upon (2nd Samuel 11:2).

The work of the Spirit is interrupted every time a believer acts upon what he sees. Anyone who believes more in the visible than the invisible will inevitably sin.

How many believers have "seen" something and based their actions on what they saw?

Eve's sin also began with sight: "And when the woman SAW that the tree was good for food..." (Genesis 3:6). She based her decision to sin on what she had seen. As a result, God's work in her was interrupted. Lot did the same thing: "And Lot lifted up his eyes, and BEHELD all the plain of Jordan" (Genesis 13:10). He also made a decision based on what he had seen; subsequently, he left the river of revival.

Achan serves as yet another example of someone whose sin was prompted by the eyes. What a wonderful revival took place at Jericho! The nation of Israel saw the walls of Jericho come tumbling down. But suddenly the revival was interrupted. Israel suffered defeat in its battle against the little city of Ai because of Achan's sin.

"When I SAW among the spoils a goodly Babylonish garment, and two hundred shekels of silver, and a wedge of gold of fifty shekels weight..." (Joshua 7:21).

Do you act upon what you see? Have you become a person who seeks money, possessions and honor? Then you are to blame for the fact that revival has died in your heart, in your family and in your surroundings.

The Sins Of The Heart

The sins of the heart are even worse than those of the eyes because God's first interest is our heart.

Let's look at some examples:

• **King Uzziah:** "And Uzziah prepared for them

throughout all the host shields, and spears and helmets, and habergeons, and bows, and slings to cast stones. And he made in Jerusalem engines, invented by cunning men, to be on the towers and upon the bulwarks, to shoot arrows and great stones withal. And his name spread far abroad; for he was marvellously helped, till he was strong. But when he was strong, his heart was lifted up to his destruction: for he transgressed against the LORD his God..." (2nd Chronicles 26:14–16).

Uzziah was blessed until he was strong and then he committed the sin of the heart: "But when he was strong, his heart was lifted up to his destruction." Therefore, his revival was interrupted.

The Lord has blessed many churches with revival. But as they have become spiritually strong, the hearts of many within those churches have become proud and self-serving. As a result, revival has been interrupted and these churches have begun to deteriorate spiritually. It is God's will to send revival when we repent—not just with our lips, but also with our hearts. Has your heart become puffed up? Pride is an abomination to the Lord; it kills His work and cuts off your "River of Life" from above.

• **King Solomon:** Another king became a casualty of the sin of the heart. The Lord loved Solomon and his fame was worldwide. But instead of giving all his love to the Lord who loved him, the Bible says: "But king Solomon loved many strange women" (1st Kings 11:1). The result of this sin of the heart was disastrous. Solomon became an idolater in his old age: "For it came to pass, when Solomon was old, that his wives turned away his heart after other gods: and his heart was not perfect with the LORD his God, as was the heart of David his father" (1st Kings 11:4).

The word "heart" occurs three times in this passage because it describes a sin of the heart. It is shattering to read these words in verse 9: "And the LORD was angry with Solomon, because his heart was turned from the LORD God of Israel, which had appeared unto him twice." Many of the Lord's servants may be praying and struggling for a revival, yet nothing happens. Why? Maybe you, too, have committed a sin of the heart. What are you bound to other than the Lord? What turns your heart toward strange gods? The Lord was angry with Solomon and had to raise up an enemy (1st Kings 11:14). Revival was over; his kingdom was divided and has remained that way until today.

The Sins Of The Tongue

The sins of the tongue are among the worst because the results are so devastating. James 3:4 speaks of big ships that are steered by small rudders. In verses 5–6 we read: "Even so the tongue is a little member, and boasteth great things. Behold, how great a matter a little fire kindleth! And the tongue is a fire, a world of iniquity: so is the tongue among our members, that it defileth the whole body, and setteth on fire the course of nature; and it is set on fire of hell."

James 4:11 reads: "Speak not evil one of another, brethren." How many children of God would break down and weep bitterly if they saw the damage that resulted because of the sins of their tongues!

In the case of Miriam and Aaron, Moses' sister and brother, we read: "And Miriam and Aaron spake against Moses because of the Ethiopian woman whom he had married: for he had married an Ethiopian woman" (Numbers 12:1). What was the result? Miriam became leprous as a punishment for speaking against one of the Lord's servants. Verse 15 says, "...Miriam was shut out from the camp seven days: and the people journeyed not till Miriam was brought in again." What a tragedy! Hundreds of thousands of believers were held up on their journey to the Promised Land because one man and one woman had sinned with their tongues.

Do you now see why the Spirit of God may not be able to break through in your heart, your family or your church? You may have prevented revival because of the sins of your tongue.

The sins of the eyes, heart and tongue all interrupt God's work and prevent a revival. Now the question arises: "Does God want to send a revival at all?" How comforting that we can find the answer to this question in the Bible. The Lord said in Ezekiel 36:26: "A new heart also will I give you, and a new spirit will I put within you: and I will take away the stony heart out of your flesh, and I will give you an heart of flesh." Notice the words "I will." The Lord will renew our hearts completely if we are willing. He will put His Spirit in our hearts so that we are full of the Holy Spirit. The Lord will also quicken a spiritually dried-up ground. God's clearly expressed will is found in Isaiah 44:3: "For I will pour water upon him that is thirsty, and floods upon the dry ground: I will pour my spirit upon thy seed, and my blessing upon thine offspring." Can God lie? Can He say something and not do it? Can He promise something and not keep His word? The Bible says that God is not a man that He should lie. Will the Lord really ignite the fire of the Spirit in and around us? The Lord Himself answered this question in Luke 12:49: "I am come to send fire on the earth; and what will I, if it be already kindled."

What Are The Divine Conditions For Revival?

• Put Away The Accursed Thing

Joshua started to pray when the defeat at Ai took place: The Lord answered in chapter 7:10: "...Get thee up; wherefore liest thou thus upon thy face?" Verse 12 says: "Therefore the children of Israel could not stand before their enemies, but turned their backs before their enemies, because they were accursed: neither will I be with you any more, except ye destroy the accursed from among you." This verse applies to each of us personally.

The children of Israel could not stand before their enemies as long as the "accursed thing" was in their midst. Neither can we stand victoriously before the enemy in our everyday lives or even hope to see revival as long as there is an "accursed thing" in our heart.

• Humble Yourself Before The Judgment Of God's Word

Let's go back to the story of David, whose lack of revival began with the lust of his eyes.

The Word of the Lord came to him through the prophet Nathan, and David became personally convicted by his words: "Thou art the man" (2nd Samuel 12:7). How did David react? He could have denied it, and he could have become angry like many of the kings after him. However, David humbled himself before the Word, which convicted him, and he confessed: "I have sinned against the LORD" (2nd Samuel 12:13). Revival could begin after he made this confession in true repentance.

We are all masters of twisting and turning in order to avoid God's Word, but the Lord says: "Thou art the man!" We have all spoken evil of others, we have sinned with our eyes, we have lied and we have been proud. The divine conditions for revival are that we humble ourselves before the Word of God and confess: "I have sinned."

• Humble Your Inner-Self

It's not only a matter of having outward humility, but also of having humility in our innermost being. The Lord said of Himself: "I am meek and lowly of heart" (Matthew 11:29).

I am convinced that the Lord is prepared to start a revival in our lives as soon as we humble our hearts with the humility that embraces all facets of our lives. A humility of understanding leads to a living faith; humility of the will leads to joyful obedience; humility of the heart leads to a mighty revival!

The Lord spoke these words in 2nd Chronicles 7:14: "If my people, which are called by my name, shall humble themselves, and pray, and seek my face, and turn from their wicked ways; then will I hear from heaven, and will forgive their sin, and will heal their land." Many people and nations in Scripture heeded God's conditions for revival, and God did send a revival. The Acts of the Apostles testify to this, as does the story of Jonah in Niniveh, which proves that a mighty revival will break out when all people humble themselves. Therefore, we cannot avoid the compelling, convicting Word of God. We must apply the divine conditions for revival now. Remember, the Lord will send a revival if we are willing!

Chapter 2

Pathway to Revival

"Awake thou that sleepest, and arise from the dead,
and Christ shall give thee light"
(Ephesians 5:14).

❦

This portion of Scripture is prophetically illustrated for us in a short story from the Old
Testament: "Now there cried a certain woman
of the wives of the sons of the prophets unto Elisha,
saying, Thy servant my husband is dead; and thou
knowest that thy servant did fear the LORD: and the
creditor is come to take unto him my two sons to be

bondmen" (2nd Kings 4:1). This widow found herself in a sorry situation. Her husband, who was a servant of the Lord, had died, and she was unable to pay her debts. When the creditor came, he wanted to take her two sons as slaves.

Second Kings 4:2–7 reveals the dialogue that took place between this woman and Elisha:

"And Elisha said unto her, What shall I do for thee? tell me, what hast thou in the house? And she said, Thine handmaid hath not anything in the house, save a pot of oil. Then he said, Go, borrow thee vessels abroad of all thy neighbours, even empty vessels; borrow not a few. And when thou art come in, thou shalt shut the door upon thee and upon thy sons, and shalt pour out into all those vessels, and thou shalt set aside that which is full. So she went from him, and shut the door upon her and upon her sons, who brought the vessels to her; and she poured out. And it came to pass, when the vessels were full, that she said unto her son, Bring me yet a vessel. And he said unto her, There is not a vessel more. And the oil stayed. Then she came and told the man of God. And he said, Go, sell the oil, and pay thy debt, and live thou and thy children of the rest."

We find three key points in this New Testament text: "Awake thou that sleepest, and arise from the dead, and Christ shall give thee light":

1) This text issues a mighty call for revival, which is more necessary today than ever. "Awake thou that sleepest!" God is sending this call throughout the

world today. He is knocking on the doors of people's hearts through the events in the Middle East. The entire situation is like a volcano that is certain to erupt unless God intercedes. However, this call is to awaken those who are sleeping because Jesus is coming!

2) This text explains the condition of those who are asleep: "arise from the dead." We mustn't forget that Paul was writing to the believers at Ephesus. The words "arise from the dead" mean to arise from amongst those who are spiritually dead. Paul was speaking to people who are physically alive, but spiritually dead.

3) This verse contains a mighty promise. Christ will give us light if we heed the call to awaken, and are willing to arise from the dead.

This story in 2nd Kings 4 concerns a woman. Why? Because the Bible says that the woman is the weaker vessel. Perhaps the Lord is saying that He reveals His strength in that which is weak.

This woman reflects three aspects of the lack of revival in our day:

A Prophetic Widow

The woman was a widow. In verse 1, she told Elisha, "Thy servant my husband is dead." To become the mother of the Messiah was the greatest hope of every Jewish woman. So widowhood placed a Jewish woman in a terrible situation because it meant she was physically incapable of realizing that hope.

One major problem within the Church today is

lack of the revelation of Jesus' glory. Where does the Church reveal the Lord's glory, reality and presence? Didn't He say, "Where two or three are gathered together in my name, there am I in the midst of them?"

Can the Church of Jesus Christ reveal Jesus to Israel in such a way as to "provoke them to jealousy"? (Romans 11:11). Israel is not in a position of conversion when it looks at today's Christianity because there is no revelation of the Messiah to be found.

Recently I received a newspaper article entitled, "Questions to a Protestant Minister" from a Swiss national newspaper. After reading it, I noticed that the Church of Jesus Christ is widowed. It said:

"One of the most important questions within Christianity seems to me to be the balance between faith and knowledge. I know that many Christians live double lives. When they hear and read reports on space travel, they think of a cold, hostile space, a vacuum, a deadly emptiness. In church, however, they sing of a heaven that is populated by hosts of angels and people who have died and gone there. This two-sidedness on the part of Christians will not be able to be kept up indefinitely. Would it not be best to do away with the term 'heaven' quietly, and take it out of the vocabulary of the Church?"

The Protestant minister answered:

"No theologian who has studied the Scripture seriously can reconcile the story of the creation of the first human beings with the doctrine of evolution and the story of the physical ascension of Christ with the knowledge of modern astronomy. Of course, heaven is no longer above and we know that human species is related to the ape. It is sheer nonsense to try and teach children in school that they simply have to believe that the earth was created in six days; I heard something of the kind being taught in a religious instruction."

This "minister" didn't even believe the Scriptures, yet he was teaching the Church.

The Church of Jesus Christ is widowed today, and God is revealing Himself in Israel. We could put it this way: The trouble with the Church is that the presence of the Lord has departed.

The Great Debt

This widowed woman was faced with a great debt. She explained that her husband was dead and that the creditor had come in 2nd Kings 4:1.

The Church is in a similar situation today. The enemy will come when the power of Jesus' victory through spiritual death has disappeared from our lives. The devil is present when Jesus is missing in one's life. On the other hand, the devil flees wherever the Lord is present.

This is a picture of the Rapture. What's becoming visible in the Church — lack of revival, spiritual death and pushing aside Christ — will be revealed at the Rapture in all of its positive and negative aspects.

The Church, which contains the true children of God, will be raptured, Satan will be thrown to the earth, and the "creditor" will have come. This prophecy is described in Revelation 12:7–9: "And there was war in heaven: Michael and his angels fought against the dragon; and the dragon fought and his angels, And prevailed not; neither was their place found any more in heaven. And the great dragon was cast out, that old serpent, called the Devil, and Satan, which deceiveth the whole world: he was cast out into the earth, and his angels were cast out with him."

When we observe believers in the Church today, we notice that this urgent claim of the "creditor" is becoming perceivable, and many have become slaves to sin. Such believers have to pay tribute to the enemy, just as Israel did in biblical times. The enemy is making his claim on believers through the lack of revival in the Church today.

This is a terrible tragedy. The new life God has given us should penetrate the world, yet it is being choked by the enemy's claims. There is no revival, but an increasing lack of it.

We see the hardness of the enemy in the ever-increasing debt which the Church has to pay. How quickly believers sin in our times! With horror I have noticed how believers who sit under the sound preaching of the Word, who are indwelt by the Holy Spirit, and whose hearts have been pierced by the Lord, so quickly return to their everyday lives, ready to sin again by backbiting, resisting admonition and correction, judging others and lying. Many lie without even thinking about it. Some are quick to believe evil and give in when the tempter comes because they have no faith resources.

Consider Exodus 32: The Lord was about to bless His people and wanted to grant them a revival, but even as He was still speaking to Moses on the mountain to give him the Law, Israel departed from Him.

God interrupted Himself in Exodus 32:7–8. Moses surely must have expected a new promise or a wonderful statement from God, but the Lord said, "Go, get thee down; for thy people, which thou broughtest out of the land of Egypt, have corrupted themselves: They have turned aside quickly out of the way which I commanded them: they have made them a molten calf, and have worshipped it, and have sacrificed thereunto, and said, These be thy gods, O Israel, which have brought thee up out of the land of Egypt." The people fell away so quickly, even as the Lord was about to bless them.

Do you realize that the Lord is very near and wants to bless us? Freedom from the power of sin is within reach. The Lord is at work on our behalf. The Holy Spirit wants to break through. The Word stands ready to be the regenerating power of our hearts, yet we manage to choose sin instead.

I am absolutely convinced that a mighty breakthrough can take place in our lives if we wait patiently for the Lord.

What would have happened had we clung persistently to Jesus and persevered in prayer? Our evil tongues, thoughts and imaginations would not be given the slightest chance to develop.

God's Children In Bondage

This widowed woman was a slave: "...and the creditor is come to take unto him my two sons to be bondmen" (2nd Kings 4:1). Here we see the enemy's claim. As God's children, we are not justified by whining because we feel so afflicted and weak. We must be honest and say, "I am in the enemy's power, I am a slave." Do we realize that we are being untruthful when we complain, hate, or think impure thoughts? That's not freedom in Christ, that's slavery! But this is the expression of a lack of revival.

This woman, a prophetic representation of the Church's situation, shows us the way out of bondage into the glorious liberty of the Cross. She broke out of her bondage into freedom! The process began the moment she did a certain thing, "Now there CRIED a certain woman of the wives of the sons of the prophets..." (2nd Kings 4:1). That's the secret! When spiritual death threatens, and the enemy is keeping us from prayer, from searching the Scriptures, and from obedience in faith, then we find ourselves in the danger of hardening our hearts and gradually becoming enslaved by this world. Revival of our hearts begin with our cry, "O my God, here I am! I can't go on like this any longer! I'm up against a wall. I'm just drifting and have become a slave to sin. I need a revival."

To whom did this woman cry? She cried to Elisha. The name "Elisha" can be translated as "my God is salvation." What did Elisha do when he heard the cry of this woman? He asked her two questions.

1. "What shall I do for thee?" That is grace, which he showed her an unlimited fullness. These words should remind us of the Lord's words to Solomon when He appeared to him in a dream: "Ask what I shall give thee" (1st Kings 3:5).

The words also bring to mind King Ahasuerus. When Esther came to him burdened with the need of her people, and she touched his scepter, the king asked, "What wilt thou, queen Esther? and what is thy request? it shall be even given thee to the half of the kingdom" (Esther 5:3). How wonderful!

When we cry out our needs in our spiritual drought and desperation, we find ourselves headed in the right direction. When we cry to God through the Lord Jesus Christ, He opens the door and asks, "What do you want? Everything is ready for you!" He promised, "Ask, and it shall be given you."

2) The second question Elisha asked was: "Tell me, what hast thou in the house?" (2nd Kings 4:2). This reveals the widow's poverty and powerlessness. On one hand she sees unlimited possibilities because Elisha is a servant of God. On the other hand, she sees that she herself has nothing: "Thine handmaid hath NOT ANYTHING in the house, save a pot of oil."

Next we see a picture of how the Lord confronts

our gaping emptiness and poverty with His wonderful fullness and riches.

This woman had nothing but a vessel (verse 2). That's exactly as much as we have. Another translation of this verse says, "I have nothing but a jar," and the Jewish Zunz Bible says, "...an anointing flask with oil." So she had but ONE vessel containing a small amount of oil.

Here the Lord begins to work on that which we still have. The Holy Spirit indwells the child of God. Perhaps you've grieved Him so much that His Spirit has withdrawn from you. But if you have the witness in your heart that you are a child of God, then you still have this empty oil flask hidden deep inside you.

Notice the mighty call for revival in verse 3. When Elisha heard that she still had a flask with oil, he said, "Go, borrow thee vessels abroad of all thy neighbours, even empty vessels; borrow not a few."

Where are the empty vessels? If you only have a little oil left, and your heart is full of envy, jealousy, criticism, unwillingness to forgive and materialism, go and find some "empty vessels." In other words, let Him empty your vessel of sin and wickedness so that He can begin His work on what is still left within you. He did great things with that small amount of oil. This has prophetic symbolism.

The Lord Jesus gives us the Holy Spirit in all His fullness when we cooperate. But the oil stands if we are not empty of ourselves: "And the oil stayed."

When the oil stands still, it's all over; but when it

flows, it reveals Jesus in His glory.

Elisha gave this woman a clear command. Not only did he tell her to fetch many empty vessels, but gave her a four-fold instruction:

1) "Come in..." (verse 4)

These words mean to come into God's presence! "Having therefore, brethren, boldness to enter into the holiest by the blood of Jesus...Let us draw near" (Hebrews 10:19–22).

2) "...shut the door upon thee"

These words contain a command to resist the devil's every influence.

3) "...and [shut the door] upon thy sons"

These words reveal an inner unity within our families.

4) "...pour out into all those vessels"

These words mean to claim in faith the fullness of the Holy Spirit.

Notice that the stagnant, but still present, oil has now suddenly been increased as long as there are empty vessels. The oil (the Holy Spirit) is in our hearts, but it's hidden deep inside.

Needless to say, if our vessels are full of wickedness, envy, unbelief and darkness, nothing will happen, because the Holy Spirit needs an "empty vessel" to work with. Jesus is not glorified as long as our vessels are not emptied of sins.

It's significant that this woman had to go to her neighbors. It is often necessary to write a letter, have a talk with someone, or ask forgiveness in order to empty our "vessels."

This was a moment of crisis for this woman, but she also took a turn for the better because she was obedient. Verse 5 says: "So she went from him, and shut the door upon her and upon her sons, who brought the vessels to her; and she poured out." Then revival came.

When we read about revival in the Bible, we notice that it always took place when the believers were obedient to the Word of God; they experienced revival when they did not remain hearers of the Word, but when they were also doers.

For example, think of King Josiah and Ezra. They began to weep when God's Law was read to them; they heeded the Word and a revival took place.

I am convinced that today's Israel is unwittingly waiting for a revival among Christians.

The oil continued to flow until there were no more empty vessels. Streams of life from above are flowing through the Holy Spirit where empty vessels are available. However, there is a warning in verse 6: "And the oil stayed" because there were no more empty vessels. The woman said to one of her sons, "Bring me yet a vessel. And he said unto her, There is not a vessel more."

Three actions can occur as a result:

• You can read this message then simply return to the order of the day.

• You can receive this message and immediately allow your thoughts to be inspired by the devil. How?

40

By thinking how wonderfully this message would suit another person.

- Or, you can grasp this message, as did this woman.

Choose the latter, because revival does not begin on a large scale, but it first occurs in the heart of an individual.

Chapter 3

How Does Revival Begin?

"Josiah was eight years old when he begin to reign, and he reigned thirty and one years in Jerusalem. And his mother's name was Jedidah, the daughter of Adaiah of Boscath. And he did that which was right in the sight of the LORD, and walked in all the way of David his father, and turned not aside to the right hand or to the left. And it came to pass in the eighteenth year of king Josiah, that the king sent Shaphan the son of Azaliah, the son of Meshullam, the scribe, to the house of the LORD, saying, Go up to Hilkiah the high priest, that he may sum the silver which is brought into the house of the LORD, which the keepers of the door have gathered of the people: And let them deliver it into the hand of the doers of the work, that have the oversight of the house of the LORD: and let them give it to the doers of the work which is in the house of the LORD, to repair the breaches of the house...And Hilkiah the high priest said unto Shaphan the scribe, I have found the book of the law in the house of the LORD. And Hilkiah gave the book to Shaphan, and he read it. And Shaphan the scribe came to the king, and brought the king word again, and said, Thy servants have gathered the money that was found in the house, and have delivered it into the hand of them that do the work, that have the oversight of the house of the LORD. And Shaphan the scribe shewed the king, saying, Hilkiah the priest hath delivered me a book. And Shaphan read it before the king. And it came to pass, when the king had heard the words of the book of the law, that he rent his clothes" (2nd Kings 22:1–5; 8–11).

"A prayer of Habakkuk the prophet upon Shigionoth. O LORD, I have heard thy speech, and was afraid: O LORD revive thy work in the midst of the years, in the midst of the years make known; in wrath remember mercy" (Habakkuk 3:1–2).

୬●

There is much ignorance today regarding revival. Therefore, it's important to tackle this subject very carefully. The first question that arises is: What kinds of people need to be revived? Revival does not begin with sinners, but with those who have been justified through faith in Jesus Christ, and have been washed in the blood of the Lamb. Habakkuk's prayer for these people was: "O LORD, revive thy work in the midst of the years."

We know that scores of lost sinners come to Jesus through revival. We also know that people are gripped by the reality of God, His holiness and majesty, and a reverent fear of God takes place through revival. We also know that believers receive a revelation of the Lamb of God that is so real that the unconverted cry out, "Lord, be merciful to me, a sinner! What must I do to be saved?" These are results of revival.

We must never be so narrow-minded as to think that conferences or crusades always produce revival. Revival may very well take place at such events, but then something else inevitably happens to interrupt the revival. Revival takes place when the Spirit of God takes over and convicts those present through the Word of God, so that believers find their first love again, and so that many others are born-again.

We all know these things, but knowing them doesn't guarantee a revival.

With heart-felt adoration we sing, "I Need Thee Every Hour," yet we go on without Him.

The tragedy is that Jesus Christ, in all of His power and glory, is not present in our churches. As a result, we start to spiritually "vegetate." There is no revival because we expect to see a revival in others. We condemn lukewarm believers, yet we forget our own hearts. Scripture is not silent on this matter:

45

"Therefore thou art inexcusable, O man, whosoever thou art that judgest: for wherein thou judgest another, thou condemnest thyself; for thou that judgest doest the same things" (Romans 2:1). Why doesn't God hear our prayers for revival? Perhaps we are hiding sin in our hearts. Second Kings 22 records the revival that took place under Josiah's leadership. This was the last revival to occur in Judah. It was as if God wanted to visit His people in mercy once again. But then the end came.

A further question also arises: Is it dangerous to be without revival? Yes! In fact, a lack of revival in God's children is PERILOUS. Why? Second Kings 22 provides the answer, which we will deal with in this chapter.

The Church of Jesus Christ still has not understood that judgment is the alternative to revival.

King Josiah, son of the godless King Manasseh, became king at the age of eight and reigned for 31 years in Jerusalem. God used him to revive His people one last time before their judgment came. Josiah was as obedient as Manasseh was godless (2nd Kings 21). This was Judah's last chance after its judgment had already been determined by God. (Notice that God's judgment upon Christianity has also been determined. We cannot avoid the judgment upon the present-day Christian world because it is fast approaching. Yet, God will send revival in the midst of judgment).

Josiah trembled and broke down as he heard the

Word of God. The book of the Law that had been found in the Temple was brought to him. Then he sent a few of his men to find a man for God, but there was none. Therefore, Josiah sent his men to the prophetess Huldah. He knew very well that they would have no revival because they were living in godlessness.

Josiah immediately saw the only alternative to revival: "Go ye, enquire of the LORD for me, and for the people, and for all Judah, concerning the words of this book that is found: for great is the WRATH OF THE LORD that is kindled against us, because our fathers have not hearkened unto the words of this book, to do according unto all that which is written concerning us" (2nd Kings 22:13). Josiah recognized the consequences of disobedience to the Word of God. He was confronted by the fact that God's wrath was upon him and his people.

Josiah recognized this and sent his men to the prophetess Huldah, "So Hilkiah the priest, and Ahikam, and Achbor, and Shaphan, and Asahiah, went unto Huldah the prophetess...And she said unto them, Thus saith the LORD God of Israel, Tell the man that sent you to me, Thus saith the LORD, Behold, I will bring evil upon this place, and upon the inhabitants thereof, even all the words of the book which the king of Judah hath read: Because they have forsaken me, and have burned incense unto other gods, that they might provoke me to anger with all the works of their hands; therefore my wrath shall be kindled against this place, and shall not be quenched" (2nd Kings 22:14; 15–17).

God confirmed exactly what Josiah heard from the Word. We also see a very moving promise in this passage. God will send a revival in the lives of individuals in the midst of His judgment: "But to the king of Judah which sent you to enquire of the LORD, thus shall ye say to him, Thus saith the LORD God of Israel. As touching the words which thou hast heard; Because thine heart was tender, and thou hast humbled thyself before the LORD, when thou heardest what I spake against this place, and against the inhabitants thereof, that they should become a desolation and a curse, and hast rent thy clothes, and wept before me; I also have heard thee, saith the LORD" (2nd Kings 22:18–19). That is both judgment and grace. This is a glorious, fascinating perspective of God's nature in the midst of apostasy. God hears those who humble themselves and will send them revival.

If we are willing, we can see just how revival begins from Josiah's example:

1. There's No Turning Back!

First, we see the young man's consistency. "And he did that which was right in the sight of the LORD, and walked in all the way of David his father, and TURNED NOT ASIDE to the right hand or to the left" (2nd Kings 22:2). We must realize what this meant for him. The land was contaminated with idolatry, impurity and the spirit of harlotry. Then suddenly someone stood up and said, "I am taking my stand against this in the Name of my Lord!"

Many are turning back today. But in Hebrews 10:38 it says, "...if any man draw back, my soul shall have no pleasure in him."

What did King Josiah do about this apostasy? He removed the houses of the harlots that were located next to the house of the Lord. Second Kings 23:7 contains a strange word written of Josiah: "And he brake down the houses of the sodomites, that were by the house of the LORD, where the women wove hangings for the grove." From these brief words, we see that harlotry was taking place very close to the sanctuary. The spirit of harlotry also prevails in the house of the Lord when women wear provocative clothing. The terrible thing is that believers, even pastors, no longer dare to open their mouths and confront the women who are guilty of this sin. Rather, they bow before the devilish dictates of fashion.

Today, people hide the wearing of such shameless clothing under the pretense of "liberty." This is hypocrisy. Women and girls who dress provocatively do not belong in the choir. Do you realize that these degenerate and shameless fashions are satanic in origin? It's not surprising that many of today's top fashion designers are sodomites. The saddest part of it is that women allow themselves to be degraded or, as Paul wrote, "...whose glory is in their shame."

A missionary in India wrote these words in a

Christian magazine: "It is well known that men are strongly attracted and tempted by things which they see. The devil, who is certainly the chief fashion designer in women's wear, knows that he can send young men to mental institutions or to an early grave by means of lust and immorality."

King Josiah was determined: HE DID NOT TURN ASIDE! That was the first step to revival. We cannot avoid this step. We must return to the Bible. We must learn to obey the Word of God again. We must tremble at God's Word again, taking it seriously and not departing from it again — even when there is tension and we are laughed at or mocked. The spirit of revival departs when believers turn aside. The spirit of harlotry breaks through mightily when the spirit of revival departs. All prayer for revival is of no avail and all prayer meetings are rendered useless. Shall we not make the basic preliminary decision in preparation for revival (this is not revival itself!) in that we say we will turn aside and depart no more? Have we divine authority? Can we still hold our ground? I have ONE support only, and ONE authority for this message: "It is written...Thus saith the Lord...." In the Name of Jesus Christ, I ask you to renounce the devilish dictates of fashion, for it is one of the worst evils in the Church of our time.

2. The Battle Is Against The Root Of All Evil

Josiah not only had all the idols broken down, but

he also removed the root of all evil: the love of money. Second Kings 22:4–7 says, "Go up to Hilkiah the high priest, that he may sum the silver which is brought into the house of the LORD, which the keepers of the door have gathered of the people: And let them deliver it into the hand of the doers of the work, that have the oversight of the house of the LORD: and let them give it to the doers of the work which is in the house of the LORD, to repair the breaches of the house, Unto carpenters, and builders, and masons, and to buy timber and hewn stone to repair the house. Howbeit there was no reckoning made with them of the money that was delivered into their hand, because they dealt faithfully."

Josiah was saying that thousands, even millions, of people are bound by the love of money. This money should have been used to beautify the house of the Lord. Don't you see how neglected the house of the Lord becomes when we hold onto our money or use it for corruptible things? We can overcome the love of money through a dedication and surrender of our financial resources to the Lord.

Believers of the New Covenant are the house of the Lord, the Church of Jesus Christ, "And the Lord added to the church daily such as should be saved" (Acts 2:47). This is a worldwide missionary enterprise. Let's do our utmost and surrender everything to the Lord so that His house will soon be completed. I believe the first step is that the love of money must be overcome in the lives of the "priests," the sanctified ones, who wear the golden plates on their foreheads engraved with the words, "Holiness to the Lord." In other words, we should never ask how much of our money we should give to the Lord, but rather how much of the Lord's money we may keep for ourselves! We are merely stewards of all He has entrusted to us. Think about what could be done in the Lord's house! A removal of the love of money from our lives would be a major step toward revival.

3. Get Back To The Bible!

When they brought the money for God's house, they found the Word of God again. Hilkiah, the high priest who brought the money, said to Shaphan the scribe: "...I have found the book of the law in the house of the LORD" (verse 8). How strange! They found the Bible again! Surely they already knew the Bible. After all, they were Jews, priests, scribes and Temple servants who lived with the Bible, and who lived in Jerusalem where the Bible was written. The answer is that as long as we do not walk in the Lord's way, and greedily hold back the Lord's money for ourselves, the Bible will remain a closed Book to us. We may be able to grasp the meaning of a few verses and find some comfort in the psalms, but the Bible will remain foreign to us.

When we start walking determinedly in the Lord's way like Josiah did, we will remove the idols from our lives. Then we, too, will "find" the Bible when we OBEY!

One would think that you could meet the Lord Himself in His house, but that is not so. The Lord will reveal Himself to those who obey Him through His Word.

Notice the conjunction "and" found in 2nd Kings 22:9–10, "And Shaphan the scribe came to the king, and brought the king word again, and said, Thy servants have gathered the money that was found in the house, and have delivered it into the hand of them that do the work, that have the oversight of the house of the LORD. And Shaphan the scribe shewed the king, saying, Hilkiah the priest hath delivered me a book. And Shaphan read it before the king" (2nd Kings 22:9–10).

Do you see this connection between obedience and a rediscovery of the Bible? We possess God's Word but are our hearts burning for Jesus? Why is revival lacking? It's not because the Bible is untrue, but because we have turned back and are holding on to sin. You may be bound by the love of money. If that is the case, stop praying for revival and the salvation of your children if you are not willing to obey His Word!

Why did all of Judah blindly follow the line of Manasseh? Judah and Benjamin served idols because the king did. The people could no longer discern for themselves because they had departed from God's Word and no longer listened to it.

When we stop listening to the Word, we swim with the tide and leave ourselves open to be used by Satan.

Judah gave herself up to harlotry and idolatry and lost her vision for the living Word.

But something wonderful followed. Not only did Israel rediscover the Bible and begin to obey, but a new blessing became visible. She heard the Word. Isn't the king's reaction relevant? "...And it came to pass, when the king had heard the words of the book of the law, that he rent his clothes" (Verse 11). This was an expression of shock, repentance, remorse and sorrow. The king's clear confession was expressed with the words, "We have sinned. The wrath of God is coming upon us." He now saw his sins as God saw them. Of course he had seen his sins before, but not as God saw them. As we read the Word of God, we will begin to see our sins as God sees them, and that is quite a shock: "...when the king had heard the words of the book of the law, that he rent his clothes."

Then the Lord gave Josiah a wonderful three-fold testimony of revival:

1) "Because thine heart was tender..." (verse 19). May our hearts also become tender! God's Word explains that the spirit of harlotry may have gotten hold of our imaginations and appearances. It may reveal that we are bound by the love of money, therefore, we are tolerating idols in our lives. When we see that God's wrath is resting upon us, our heart will become tender. This can be the beginning of a mighty revival, not only in our own lives, but also in the lives of our families and church members.

2) "...and wept before me" (verse 19). King Josiah cried. He had done wrong and was corrupt, but he allowed his heart be made tender; he humbled himself and wept before the Lord.

3) Therefore the Lord said, "I have also heard thee." Thus the revival has three effects that reflect the glory of the Lamb in the midst of apostasy. The result was that the Passover Lamb was made visible again, "And the king commanded all the people, saying, Keep the passover unto the LORD your God, as it is written in the book of this covenant. Surely there was not holden such a passover from the days of the judges that judged Israel, nor in all the days of the kings of Israel, nor of the kings of Judah; But in the eighteenth year of king Josiah, wherein this passover was holden to the LORD in Jerusalem" (2nd Kings 23:21–23).

Josiah's attitude was given a distinction to which I have not found an equal in all of the Old Testament, "And like unto him was there no king before him, that turned to the LORD with all his heart, and with all his soul, and with all his might, according to all the law of Moses; neither after him arose there any like him" (verse 25). That was why the Lord heard him.

We are now in a glorious, yet dangerous position. It is glorious because the Word applies to us: "Seek ye the LORD while he may be found, call ye upon him while he is near" (Isaiah 55:6). This is glorious if we heed it. Then we will be revived. We must recognize our sins so that something new can begin in our lives as a child of God.

The danger is that we become even more hardened, for if you say no now, when will you say yes? It is God's grace that He afflicts us and speaks to us in this way today. Therefore, "O earth, earth, earth, hear the word of the LORD...He that hath an ear, let him hear what the Spirit saith unto the churches" (Jeremiah 22:29; Revelation 2:29).

Chapter 4

Does God Want To Send
A Revival?

"If I shut up heaven that there be no rain, or if
I command the locusts to devour the land, or if
I send pestilence among my people; If my people,
which are called by my name, shall humble themselves,
and pray, and seek my face, and turn from
their wicked ways; then will I hear from heaven, and will
forgive their sin, and will heal their land"
(2nd Chronicles 7:13–14).

ॐ

Some believers think that the Lord will not send
any more revival. Therefore we must ask: Do
we have any reason to believe that revival is
really God's will?

Also important is to seek God's will for our own personal lives. A person can only be truly happy when he lives within the realm of God's will. We can miss God's first and best when we avoid His will through our disobedience.

What Is God's Will?

How can we know God's will? Here are three ways:

1. He reveals His will through the leading of the Holy Spirit. The Lord said that the Holy Spirit would lead us into all truth. All who truly want to be led know the way. The Spirit of God leads us. I have often spoken with believers who are constantly struggling with conflicts: "Is this the way I should go? I don't know if it's the Lord's will." Such a person is not walking in His way. We will never go wrong when we desire to have the Lord's will performed in our lives. If we find ourselves headed in the wrong direction, the Lord will bring us back and say, "Not that way — this way!" In other words, He will make His will known to us.

2. He reveals His will through circumstances. He can lead us into certain situations that enable us to recognize His will.

3. He reveals His will to us in His Word. For example, we know God's will concerning the salvation of all men. If we ask whether God wants everyone to be saved, we only have to turn to 1st Timothy 2:4 to find our answer: "...Who will have all men to be saved,

and to come unto the knowledge of the truth." Here we are given great insight into God's will. God wants to save all men. If a person thinks that he cannot be saved because of his many sins, it is only a suggestion of the devil, for God loves the sinner in Jesus Christ, who shed His blood on Calvary's Cross. While our sins separate us from God, confession to the Lord cleanses us and brings us into the realm of God's will.

His Will Is Our Sanctification

We also know God's will concerning our sanctification: "For this is the will of God, even your sanctification" (1st Thessalonians 4:3). What does sanctification actually mean? Sanctification is our personal appropriation of the redemption that took place through Jesus. This means not only the forgiveness of our sins, but also the renewal of our lives. In other words, sanctification is a step beyond forgiveness of sins. Forgiveness means that we are pardoned from our sins. Sanctification encompasses our walk with the Lord. Our sanctification is a growth process that will continue until the day we die. However, we can choose to ignore our sanctification by participating in sinful behavior.

Two Ways

We have two options: Experience God's blessing and comfort when we remain in His will, or find ourselves within the sphere of Satan's will. This point is found in 2nd Timothy 2:26: "...out of the snare of the devil, who are taken captive by him at his will."

Many are not ruled by God's will, but by Satan's. They have to do things that they do not want to do. They give in to their passions although they do not want to; they lie although they want to speak the truth; and they are impure although they would like to be pure. If this describes you, then you are ruled by Satan.

Water And Fire

Two biblical symbols that point to revival are water and fire.

Ezekiel 47 says that living waters flowed from the Temple of the Lord and flooded the land. Verse 9 says that new life is brought about wherever that water flows. This also reminds us of Exodus 17, when the Israelites were thirsty and Moses struck the rock and living water flowed from it. As a result, Israel awoke to new life. This is a picture of revival!

The Lord spoke of a revived people in John 7:38: "He that believeth on me, as the scripture hath said, out of his belly shall flow rivers of living water."

Fire is also a picture of revival. This is obvious from Acts 2, which describes the greatest revival of all times: the birth of the Church. "Tongues like as of fire" were on the heads of the believers. The Gospel was preached in power.

The Bible clearly reveals God's will concerning water and fire. God said of the water: "For I will pour water upon him that is thirsty, and floods upon the dry ground…" (Isaiah 44:3).

Regarding the fire, Jesus said: "I am come to send fire on the earth; and what will I, if it be already kindled?" How clearly God's will regarding revival is shown to us!

Endtimes Fire

Nevertheless, many believers say, "But we are living in the endtimes today." That's true, but the Lord has also revealed His will for the endtimes.

In the Old Testament book of Joel we find these moving words: "And rend your heart, and not your garments, and turn unto the LORD your God: for he is gracious and merciful, slow to anger, and of great kindness, and repenteth him of the evil…Let the priests, the ministers of the LORD, weep between the porch and the altar, and let them say, Spare thy people, O LORD, and give not thine heritage to reproach, that the heathen should rule over them…" (Joel 2:13,17). That was a call to revival.

As New Testament believers, we have become priests of the LORD. This wonderful promise is found in Joel 2:23: "…Be glad then, ye children of Zion, and rejoice in the LORD your God: for he hath given you the former rain moderately, and he will cause to come down for you the rain, the former rain, and the latter rain." When will this happen? "For, behold, in those days, and in that time, when I shall bring again the captivity of Judah and Jerusalem, I will also gather all nations and will bring them down into the valley of Jehoshaphat, and will plead with them there for my people and for my heritage Israel, whom they have scattered among the nations, and parted my land" (Joel 3:1–2). This refers to our present day! We are seeing how the Lord is blessing Judah and Jerusalem. He is leading His people back to the land of their fathers although they are still not saved.

We can also see how God's judgment upon the Gentiles is approaching because of His people. Therefore, these endtimes have the promise that God most certainly does want to send revival.

The Need For Revival

If God wants to send a revival, then why doesn't it come? In order to answer this question, we first must know what revival actually is. To be "revived" is to be "awakened." Thus, the necessity for revival, or an awakening, presupposes a condition of sleep. That is why the Apostle Paul exclaimed these words in Ephesians 5:14: "Awake thou that sleepest, and arise from the dead, and Christ shall give thee light."

Have you fallen prey to this fatal, spiritual sleep? This can be determined by your concern for the needs of a lost world. Many believers have gone to sleep and do not realize what is going on around them; they are blind and deaf. To put it in biblical terms, they are rich and have a need for nothing. This is what the risen Lord said in Revelation 3:17: "Because thou sayest, I am rich, and increased with goods, and have need of nothing; and knowest not that thou art wretched, and miserable, and poor, and blind, and naked...." Wake up! To be awakened means to be revived; it means to see our sins as God sees them. The result is repentance, which is followed by revival.

Revival Is Not A Miracle

We must also know what revival is not. It's not a miracle of God. Many Christians think that revival is God's wonderful intervention. If that were the case, we wouldn't have to worry about it. In other words, we would have no responsibility in the matter of revival because everything would depend upon God.

In this connection, we are continually confronted with a misused Bible verse. John 3:8 says, "The wind bloweth where it listeth, and thou hearest the sound thereof, but canst not tell whence it cometh, and whither it goeth: so is every one that is born of the Spirit." That doesn't mean it's up to God to revive us while we remain inactive. Jesus used this illustration to show how a person is regenerated. That, of course, is a miracle.

God does want to send revival, but not by supernatural power. He will send a revival when we are willing to use the means that have been given us. If you are not revived, it is because deep down, you really don't want to be.

Many believers are unaware of this because they don't know their own disobedient hearts. But our hearts are like a field that we must work with if we expect to harvest fruit.

Can a farmer look at his field and say, "I'm just going to wait until God does a miracle and makes something grow!" Of course, God has to give growth, but the farmer has to do his share. He has to plow the ground and sow the seed. If he does his share, God will bless him and send rain so that he will bring in a great harvest.

Break Up The Fallow Ground

Now we come to a sore point that even many in Gospel-preaching churches do not want to hear. Jeremiah 4:3 reads: "Break up your fallow ground, and sow not among thorns." The Lord wants us to examine ourselves before His holy face. He wants to search our hearts so that we will not "...sow...among thorns." We are expected to plow new ground.

In this connection, the words found in Hosea have deeply impressed me: "...break up your fallow ground: for it is time to seek the LORD, till he come and rain righteousness upon you" (Hosea 10:12). Responsibility for revival in our families and churches begins with the individual believer. God wants to send revival. The question is whether we really want it or not.

Here are six reasons revival must take place in our time:

1. Only a revival can make Jesus' resurrection a reality to the world.

How did Jesus prove that He really was the Son of

God? Romans 1:4 explains how: "And declared to be the Son of God with power, according to the spirit of holiness, by the resurrection from the dead." How do we prove to the world that Jesus Christ has risen from the dead? We demonstrate it by a life that has been revived.

Nothing is more damnable than a "dead" Christianity. The Lord prefers heathens to half-hearted, lukewarm Christians. He abhors them and even says: "So then because thou art lukewarm, and neither cold nor hot, I will spue thee out of my mouth" (Revelation 3:16). This is why it is so urgent that the life of Christ is revealed through us. That is revival, and that is how we prove to the world that Jesus lives! "And ye shall find me, when ye shall search for me with all your heart. And I will be found of you, saith the Lord."

2. Only true revival can produce the unity Jesus prayed for in John 17.

To be revived also means that we love our brethren through the Lord Jesus. Love is the greatest gift; it is able to overcome disunity. Jesus said: "...Thou shalt love the Lord thy God with all thy heart, and with all thy soul, and with all thy mind. This is the first and great commandment. And the second is like unto it, Thou shalt love thy neighbour as thyself. On these two commandments hang all the law and the prophets" (Matthew 22:37–40).

3. Only revival can postpone the threatening judgment.

Brothers and sisters, it is much later than we may think! Dark, ominous clouds of judgment are hanging over the world and can burst at any moment.

However, threatening clouds of judgment are also hanging over the Church of Jesus Christ. These clouds can only be averted by revival. This becomes painfully clear when we read Revelation 2:5: "Remember therefore from whence thou art fallen, and repent, and do the first works; or else I will come unto thee quickly, and will remove thy candlestick out of his place, except thou repent." The Lord is giving the Church an ultimatum: Revival or judgment? The Lord is calling the world to repentance and His Church to revival. If we ignore His call, we will find ourselves objects of His judgment.

We only need to look around to see the spiritual decay in so many churches. Thankfully, there are exceptions. How did this modern, damnable "theology" find its way into our churches? This "theology" that denies Jesus was and is the Son of God, that He was born of the virgin Mary, that He publicly demonstrated innumerable miracles, that He died on Calvary's Cross and that He physically arose on the third day?

It is literally the work of demons when pastors no longer believe that the Bible is the Word of God and deny the resurrection of Christ. Is it by chance that sleep comes over you even before you enter such a church? This is the terrible judgment that has come upon both the pastors and churches because the Lord has removed their candlestick since there was, and is, no repentance.

We see the same circumstances within many families. Some "Christian" families have become so spiritually dark that their children would rather go out into the world because they do not know the Word of God. Why? Because their parents are not willing to repent. That is why I say to you now: Repent so that revival can take place!

Let's consider Jesus' words recorded in Matthew 5:13: "Ye are the salt of the earth: but if the salt have lost his savour, wherewith shall it be salted? it is thenceforth good for nothing, but to be cast out, and to be trodden under foot of men." Isn't that the case today? Yes, we hold crusades and "revivals" and we call on "specialists" to come and stimulate the life of the Church, but there is no power to bring about a new birth. There may be many "converts," but they will soon fall away. Why? Because the powers of death are present, keeping the Church of Jesus Christ from giving birth to spiritual children. The Lord Jesus spoke of this in John 8:21: "Then said Jesus again unto them, I go my way, and ye shall seek me, and shall die in your sins."

The last part of Jesus' statement is frightening: "...and shall die in your sins." We must face this truth. We don't need new methods, nor do we need to adapt ourselves to modern viewpoints. What we need is a good old-fashioned revival. When revival takes place, spiritually empowered men and women of prayer will be awakened, and they will cry out to God so that darkness is banished. When revival takes place, a cleansing from sin occurs and spiritual weakness disappears. When revival takes place, the curse is changed into blessing. God wants to give us joy if we allow ourselves to be revived.

We can reject this message, but we must know that we will become a stumbling stone for revival in the Church if we do so. If we say yes and humble ourselves by confessing, "Yes, my God, I am in the way. I have lost my first love, but I want to break up my fallow ground," then the Lord will answer by starting a revival within us; subsequently, others will be revived through us.

4. Revival can make the Word of God a way of life to the godless.

Haven't you noticed that the world is becoming more and more indifferent to a tract or sermon? Have you experienced that it is increasingly difficult to share the Gospel with someone? It used to be quite different, but today it is often like talking to a wall. Many Christians say that it's because people are hardening their hearts, but I don't think so; I believe the Church is becoming harder and harder. The longer revival is delayed through disobedience, the more powerless our testimonies become. If a child of God does not experience periods of deep contrition, deep repentance and cleansing, then he is already hardened; he is a pseudo-Christian and his testimony is powerless. The world laughs at such Christians.

Why did the people laugh at Lot when he said: "Up, get you out of this place; for the LORD will destroy this city. But he seemed as one that mocked unto his sons in law" (Genesis 19:14)? Because Lot was a hardened man who was full of compromises.

Why aren't your children converted? Is it because of their schools or the terrible spirit of these times? No! It is because you are not revived. Your children will not be converted by attending Sunday school. They will not be converted because you read a Bible verse to them every day, or because you force them to go to church with you. They will be converted when you are revived and when they see Jesus in you. Then the atmosphere will be charged with the Holy Spirit.

5. Revival will enable you to progress in your sanctification.

So many believers are in a spiritual "rut." They pray and receive the Word, but they do not make any progress in their sanctification. This is sad. If we remain as we are, if we are not more deeply sanctified, we who receive the Word of God with our minds without digesting it in the spirit through humility and cleansing will become complacent. We will become spiritually dull.

The Lord Himself spoke of this in His lament through the prophet Hosea: "...my people are bent to backsliding from me: though they called them to the most High, none at all would exalt him" (Hosea 11:7). Those who are revived are willing to be broken and enter lives of even deeper obedience. As a result, such a person begins to make progress in their sanctification.

6. Revival will hasten Jesus' return.

When true revival takes place in God's children — and this has to begin in the believer because the Bible says that judgment begins with the house of God — then people who have never heard the Gospel will suddenly be gripped by it. No longer will it be difficult to evangelize. We will not have to call in evangelists to hold special crusades and revivals because believers themselves will evangelize. This was the case in the Acts of the Apostles: The believers were so full of the Holy Spirit that they went to their neighbors and implored them to come to Jesus.

Luke 14:23 reads: "Go out into the highways and hedges, and compel them to come in." In other words, we must convince unbelievers of their need for Jesus. When revival comes, the number of born-again believers will have grown; thus the fullness of the Gentiles will be hastened. The Bible says that Jesus will return when the full number of the Church from among the Gentiles has become a fact. The Church of Jesus Christ holds a definite number of members, just as the stars are also numbered: "He telleth the number of the stars; he calleth them all by their names" (Psalm 147:4). Jesus' return will be hastened the moment the miracle of conversion takes place.

Revival Will Lead To Israel

God has prepared everything. All of His actions

press toward His goal. Romans 11:25 says, "...blindness in part is happened to Israel, until the fulness of the Gentiles be come in." This means that Israel will be blind for her Messiah until the last of the Gentiles is converted! Today we see Israel's reestablishment. Many Jews are now reading the New Testament; their blindness is beginning to lift. Only one thing is lacking for the return of Jesus to take place: The fullness of the Gentiles! Why? Because there is no revival.

Jesus spoke of the Gentiles who would believe in Him in John 10:16: "And other sheep I have, which are not of this fold: them also I must bring, and they shall hear my voice; and there shall be ONE fold, and ONE shepherd." The coming of Jesus and the urgent need for revival go hand in hand.

A mighty revival will take place as soon as three things happen:

1) When God's children finally become willing to be a whole offering. What does it mean to be a whole offering? Paul spoke of this in Romans 12:1: "I beseech you therefore...that ye present your bodies a living sacrifice, holy, acceptable unto God." That means everything — hands, feet, eyes, ears, heart, mind, time, energy, face — must be on the altar, completely and unconditionally.

The trouble today is the deterioration in the quality of our devotion or theoretical surrender to Jesus. Very few Christians have really laid themselves upon the altar. We sing, "My Jesus, I love thee..." and "All to Jesus I Surrender...", but it becomes hypocrisy before God and man if we hide things in our hearts that we are unwilling to give up.

I do not know what it happens to be in your case, but you do, and so does God: "...man looketh on the outward appearance, but the LORD looketh on the heart"(1st Samuel 16:7).

Judgment In The Church

Ananias and Sapphira were hypocrites (Acts 5). They brought their gifts to the apostle's feet but Peter said, "...Ananias, why hath Satan filled thine heart to lie to the Holy Ghost, and to keep back part of the price of the land? Whiles it remained, was it not thine own? and after it was sold, was it not in thine own power? why hast thou conceived this thing in thine heart? thou hast not lied unto men, but unto God. And Ananias hearing these words fell down, and gave up the ghost" (verses 3–5a). What had this man done? Yes, he gave a large donation, but he was also a hypocrite! He behaved as though he had given the Lord everything, a "whole offering," but in reality, this was not so.

Many believers today do the same, and this is holding up revival! With words, gestures and actions, appearances are produced that do not correspond with reality. You can only be one or the other, a hypocrite or a whole offering.

2) We will see revival when a whole offering is sacrificed. As we warned at the beginning of this chapter, we will weep over the plight of a lost world. Then

at last we will pray: "I will not let thee go except thou bless me." This crying before the Lord cannot be produced, but the Lord will grant it when we obey Him. If you have never wept over the sins of God's people and over lost sinners, then you are not yet revived yourself.

3) We may expect revival when we no longer resist the truth: "If my people, which are called by my name, shall humble themselves, and pray, and seek my face, and turn from their wicked ways; then will I hear from heaven, and will forgive their sin, and will heal their land" (2nd Chronicles 7:14). Can God say something and not do it? He says: "If YOU are willing, I am too. If you humble yourself and pray, then I will hear you from heaven." He lives; our God lives! Will you confess your sins to Him? Will you surrender that to Him that you should have surrendered way back when? Will you break from those sins you should have broken from long ago? Will you do it now? If not, the earnest Word of the Lord will apply to you: "I will remove thy candlestick."

Chapter 5

What Is Our Calling?

"For, brethren, ye have been called unto liberty; only use not liberty for an occasion to the flesh, but by love serve one another. For all the law is fulfilled in one word, even in this; Thou shalt love thy neighbour as thyself. But if ye bite and devour one another, take heed that ye be not consumed one of another. This I say then, Walk in the Spirit, and ye shall not fulfil the lust of the flesh. For the flesh lusteth against the Spirit, and the Spirit against the flesh: and these are contrary the one to the other: so that ye cannot do the things that ye would. But if ye be led of the Spirit, ye are not under the law" (Galatians 5:13–18).

❧

Prayer and revival are inseparable. Wherever a revival takes place, it has been preceded by prayer; wherever there is prayer in Spirit and in truth, revival inevitably follows. If such is not the case, then it may be logical to assume that the prayer may have been offered with questionable motives. When revivals fail to produce lasting fruit, then we can be sure that they were not a genuine revival.

A careful examination of Galatians 5:13 answers the question of our calling. Born-again believers are called to liberty! The Apostle Paul said: "Because the creature itself also shall be delivered from the bondage of corruption into the glorious liberty of the children of God" (Romans 8:21). A born-again person is released from the bondage of sin, the yoke of the Law; subsequently, he attains glorious liberty as a child of God. He is now free from the pressure and curse of the Law; he's free from the guilt of past transgressions, and he is now a free son (or daughter) of the Living God.

But Paul also referred to the dangers that can occur when this liberty is misused: "...only use not liberty for an occasion to the flesh" (Galatians 5:13).

Holy Spirit Leadership

What are we expected to do with the wonderful liberty we have in Christ Jesus? Can we continue to live for ourselves? No! Our newly received liberty must be completely subject to the Spirit of God: "But if ye be led of the Spirit, ye are not under the law"

(Galatians 5:18). Therefore, we do not use this liberty at our own discretion, but at the discretion of the Spirit of God. This may be easy to say, but we must also put it into practice. In our flesh we are opponents to the Holy Spirit's ruling in our lives. All that our human bodies and minds contain is sin. The Bible says: "For the flesh lusteth against the Spirit, and the Spirit against the flesh: and these are contrary the one to the other: so that ye cannot do the things that ye would" (Galatians 5:17). It's very simple: We are either ruled by the Spirit or by our flesh.

Why does it take so long for the Holy Spirit to take leadership in the lives of many believers? An illustration from the world of politics may help us understand. Many countries are incapable of installing a practical government because they don't have a political party that carries a large enough majority. Similarly, the Holy Spirit's rulership in the lives of Christians may be stifled because the majority-vote in their hearts may be lacking. That is also one of the reasons for the ups and downs they experience.

We inevitably are subject to many different influences, including our feelings. However, if we allow ourselves to be taken over by our feelings, it is because the Spirit of God is not ruling in us. Our inner discord is caused by various sins, such as pride, envy, dogmatism, gossip or other evil passions, that we allow to govern our lives.

The Holy Spirit is not a dictator! He wants to rule in us but will withdraw when we doubt. Conflicts result when we don't allow the Holy Spirit to rule our hearts. Spiritual and carnal Christians do not get along with one another. Ultimately, a separation must take place: "But if ye bite and devour one another, take heed that ye be not consumed one of another" (Galatians 5:15). "Biting" and "devouring" can also occur in our thoughts by means of grudges, criticism and mistrust, making the Christian life seem like a continual struggle and turning discipleship into great effort. This is exactly the opposite of what Galatians 5:18 says: "But if ye be led of the Spirit, ye are not under the law." When the Spirit of God is able to rule over us, then there will be no compulsion or struggle, just glorious peace.

The Lord Is The Spirit

Important to remember is that just as the Spirit rules over our lives, the Lord also is ruling over us: "Now the Lord is that Spirit: and where the Spirit of the Lord is, there is liberty" (2nd Corinthians 3:17). The person whose heart is ruled by the Holy Spirit has the wonderful liberty of approaching the very throne of God in prayer. This is one way we can tell how much control the Spirit of God has in our lives. Many pray by searching for fancy words and believing that "longer is better." Others believe they have to use "religious" phrases. But when the Holy Spirit rules our lives, Romans 8:26 becomes a reality: "...for we know not what we should pray for as we ought: but the Spirit itself maketh intercession for us with groanings which cannot be uttered." Our prayer lives will have only as much impact and power as the extent to which the Spirit of God rules in us.

We have all experienced the spirit of fear, which does its best to drag us down; however, there is also a spirit of liberty which, through the blood of Christ, draws us upward and leads us into God's presence: "For the law of the Spirit of life in Christ Jesus hath made me free from the law of sin and death" (Romans 8:2).

There are two laws: 1) The law of sin and death, which regards our bodies; and 2) the law of the Spirit of life in Christ Jesus. Which law is stronger? It depends on who we allow to govern our lives. Without the Holy Spirit's rule in our lives, prayer will always be impotent and egocentric. Victorious prayer will not take place because we will have taken God off the throne and replaced Him with idols such as pride and egotism. However, when the Spirit of God rules, we become priestly in our prayers, we can meet the enemy like kings, and we can come before the Father as His son or daughter!

God Never Repeats Himself

Perhaps you have become spiritually impotent. This, we know, is the devil's goal. Do you want to experience the power of prayer in a new way? Of course you do. We all want to pray faithfully and per-severingly. Here's how: God opens the heavens and shows us things we don't even know if we accept His invitation: "Call unto me, and I will answer thee, and shew thee great and mighty things, which thou knowest not" (Jeremiah 33:3).

When we pray in a manner that is conscious of the Holy Spirit's leading, the Lord shows us His answer in wonderful ways that we've never even dreamed of. I am only saying this based on what Scripture says and how it has been true in my own life. That is why I am convinced that the Lord has blessings prepared for us, blessings the likes of which we have not the slightest idea, because God never repeats Himself!

For this reason, we must never compare reports of past revivals with how He may choose to work today. The Bible says that God's mercies are **new** every morning. But we need to make sure that we allow the Holy Spirit to lead our prayer lives. As I mentioned earlier, that can only happen when the Holy Spirit rules our lives. If we really want revival, we must surrender our power to the One who purchased us. We must not allow ourselves to be driven by the flesh. The Lord is not interested in lip service. We have the opportunity of demonstrating this complete surrender with humility in our daily lives.

Chapter 6

Seven Aspects Of Prayer

"Hear me when I call, O God of my righteousness:
thou hast enlarged me when I was in distress; have
mercy upon me, and hear my prayer"
(Psalm 4:1).

❧

In this psalm, David asked the Lord to hear his
prayer the very moment he called on Him. He
didn't imagine that the Lord would do even
more, for it is written: "Before they call, I will
answer." We must realize that the Lord knows the
answers to our prayers before we even know our own

needs. If it is true that the Holy Spirit prays through us (Romans 8:26), then the requests are not ours, but God's, which He wants to bring to pass. Therefore, when the Holy Spirit is able to pray through us, the answer is virtually guaranteed. For this reason, we cannot say enough about what prayer really is, but let's consider seven aspects of it:

1. Are We Ready To Receive?

Romans 8:26 says: "...for we know not what we should pray for as we ought: but the Spirit itself maketh intercession for us with groanings which cannot be uttered" (Romans 8:26). The Holy Spirit passes to us what God wants to give; thus, we must be ready to receive the Holy Spirit. Many will protest because, as believers, we already have the Holy Spirit. That is true. However we may not be full of the Holy Spirit. So we need to always be ready to receive a new filling of the Holy Spirit that God has prepared for us.

How can we express our readiness? "These all continued with one accord in prayer and supplication, with the women, and Mary the mother of Jesus, and with his brethren" (Acts 1:14). This is the foundation: an inner readiness that's necessary in order to receive the Holy Spirit's filling.

2. Are We Ready For The Whole Truth?

It is pointless to hold prayer meetings if not everyone is ready to hear or receive the whole truth: "Let us draw near with a true heart..." (Hebrews 10:22).

The Apostle John also referred to this: "My little children, let us not love in word, neither in tongue; but in deed and in truth. And hereby we know that we are of the truth, and shall assure our hearts before him" (1st John 3:18–19). In other words, if we are in the truth and live what we profess to believe, then our hearts can be assured before Him in prayer. We will then be able to rest in Him who is the truth, and will be able to break through in prayer. Many believers never break through into the inner sanctuary because the door is closed to them. They pray, but they are relieved when they can say "Amen." If that's the case, something is blocking their communication with heaven. They may not be ready for the whole truth about themselves.

3. Are We Ready To Believe?

The word "faith" has little meaning today simply because it is seen in so few believers. Yet it is very real and alive. We can attain anything through faith: "But without faith it is impossible to please him: for he that cometh to God must believe that he is, and that he is a rewarder of them that diligently seek him" (Hebrews 11:6).

This closely relates to our being ready to receive the whole truth. When we are not prepared to receive the truth, our faith will be equally lacking. The faith that is found in our hearts is just as strong as the truth found within us.

Hebrews 10:22 reveals a connection in this regard:

"Let us draw near with a true heart in full assurance of faith...." In other words, we are unable to believe when we are not in the truth.

Our prayers will not be true if we vainly cling to other things while we try to seek the Lord's face. Such prayers have no power, because if we are liars, we cannot have faith.

We can possess the great territories before us because all things are possible for those who believe. How can we possess them? Through prayer!

Isn't it strange that we pray for revival and many other things, yet we are full of unbelief! This clearly was a characteristic of the first church in Jerusalem: "Peter therefore was kept in prison: but prayer was made without ceasing of the church unto God for him" (Acts 12:5). The members of the Church prayed diligently for Peter's release from prison, and God answered them. But how did they react? "And as Peter knocked at the door of the gate, a damsel came to hearken, named Rhoda. And when she knew Peter's voice, she opened not the gate for gladness, but ran in, and told how Peter stood before the gate. And they said unto her, Thou art mad" (Acts 12:13–15). Their unbelief was the measure of their faith: "Then said they, It is his angel" (Acts 12:15).

Herein lies the reason that we do not break through. So many prayer meetings take place throughout the country, yet there is no revival because the readiness to receive, the readiness for the whole truth, and the readiness to believe are not present.

4. Are We Ready To Have Our Souls Searched?

Nothing searches our soul more than prayer. I can say this from my own experience. When we come into God's holy presence through prayer, He searches our innermost being and reveals everything. If there is any hindrance, God does not accept our saying, "Lord, if there is any hindrance in me, take it away." When something is in us that ought not be there, the Lord will put His finger on it and identify why we cannot get through to Him.

This is evident in Joshua 7:6: "And Joshua rent his clothes, and fell to the earth upon his face before the ark of the LORD until the eventide, he and the elders of Israel, and put dust upon their heads." We must be ready to let the Lord search our hearts: "And the LORD said unto Joshua, Get thee up; wherefore liest thou thus upon thy face?" (Joshua 7:10). Only when we cease our pious talk and religious chatter will be ready for the Lord to search our hearts. Is there pride, envy, jealousy, hatred or irreconciliation in your life? There is no point in going to a prayer meeting if you do not have this readiness. True prayer involves a readiness to be searched.

5. Are We Ready To Be Reconciled?

Irreconciliation is one characteristic of the endtime Christian (2nd Timothy 3:3). The Lord will close the heavens over us if we do not forgive those who have wronged us. If we are not ready to forgive other people, we may as well stop praying.

Perhaps you've done something harmful to someone. Maybe you just don't like that person, or you have something against him or her. Scripture says that when you pray, then you should also forgive: "And when ye stand praying, forgive, if ye have ought against any: that your Father also which is in heaven may forgive you your trespasses" (Mark 11:25).

We must always be mindful that we will experience forgiveness only to the extent that we are willing to forgive others, "And forgive us our debts, as we forgive our debtors" (Matthew 6:12).

It is pointless to pray for revival if we are not ready to get to the core of the matter so that the Living Lord can reveal Himself, and pour out His Spirit for revival. We must go the whole way or we will become lukewarm. Our prayer meetings will become sanctimonious.

The world is looking for people like the first disciples, who were full of the Holy Spirit, firm in their faith, and reconciled to one another. Then we can pray and the Lord will answer.

The Lord shows us the way in Isaiah 58:6–9: "Is not this the fast that I have chosen? to loose the bands of wickedness, to undo the heavy burdens, and to let the oppressed go free, and that ye break every yoke? Is it not to deal thy bread to the hungry, and that thou bring the poor that are cast out to thy house? when thou seest the naked, that thou cover him; and that thou hide not thyself from thine own flesh? Then shall thy light break forth as the morning, and thine health shall spring forth speedily: and thy righteousness shall go before thee; the glory of the LORD shall be thy reward. Then shalt thou call, and the LORD shall answer; thou shalt cry, and he shall say, Here I am. If thou take away from the midst of thee the yoke, the putting forth of the finger, and speaking vanity." The path to revival is revealed to us, but are we willing to go that way?

6. Are We Ready To Take?

What do I mean by being "ready to take"? John revealed a condition: "And whatsoever we ask, we receive of him, because we keep his commandments, and do those things that are pleasing in his sight" (1st John 3:22). In other words, our ability to receive God's blessings depends on our obedience. Our readiness to take what we pray for will be present when we pray as He directs.

A person who is obedient and prays in such a way is indescribably rich and will be able to say with King David: "My cup runneth over." He also will be able to rejoice with Paul: "Blessed be the God and Father of our Lord Jesus Christ, who hath blessed us with all spiritual blessings in heavenly places in Christ" (Ephesians 1:3).

7. Are We Ready For A Completely New, Worldwide And Glorious Commission?

Let the words of the Lord to His servant Ananias

when He sent him to Saul of Tarsus serve as a reminder: "...Arise, and go into the street, which is called Straight, and enquire in the house of Judas for one called Saul of Tarsus: for, behold, he prayeth" (Acts 9:11). This man prayed and God gave him a commission that has affected the world until this present day. Paul must have prayed mightily after his conversion. In fact, he asked, "Lord, what wilt thou have me to do?" Paul completely surrendered his will to the Lord. The Lord also has a new commission for us when we pray like Saul, expressing our readiness.

Chapter 7

How To Prepare For Victorious Prayer

"From whence come wars and fightings among you? come they not hence, even of your lusts that war in your members? Ye lust, and have not: ye kill, and desire to have, and cannot obtain: ye fight and war, yet ye have not, because ye ask not. Ye ask, and receive not, because ye ask amiss, that ye may consume it upon your lusts" (James 4:1–3).

✳

W hen believers come together to pray, which is a commendable practice, it is important for them to consider the purpose of their meeting. Is there any promise for such a prayer meeting? Will the Lord hear and answer their prayers?

The Key

According to Scripture, every promise contained in the Bible has a key we must use before we can claim it. This key is called "obedience in faith." We must use this key before we do anything else. Notice that this key is not only faith, but it's obedience in faith.

We just read: "Ye ask, and receive not." What is the reason for this powerlessness and inability to receive? In his first letter, the Apostle John wrote: "...whatsoever we ask, we receive of him" (1st John 3:22a). Therefore, we have the power to receive answers to our prayers in faith.

However, something else is written in James 4:3: "Ye ask, and receive not." Why? Because the motives in our hearts are not pure and clear: "...because ye ask amiss, that ye may consume it upon your lusts." In other words, we don't receive answers to our prayers when our motives for prayer don't focus on Jesus and Jesus alone.

Consider the brethren who prayed in an upper room in Jerusalem after Pentecost. I believe there were only a few of them, but their prayers caused the house to be shaken and God to answer in a miraculous way. Why? Because all obstacles had been removed.

Now let us look at four obstacles that must be

removed if believers are to pray in one accord so that the things that take place will be done so to the honor and glory of the Lord.

1. Ye Ask, And Receive Not

I believe that our egos take up more space than Christ in our spiritual lives. We see this at the end of James 4:3: "...that ye may consume it upon your lusts."

In theory, we know what Scripture says about being crucified. We also know that Galatians 2:19–20 says: "For I through the law am dead to the law, that I might live unto God. I am crucified with Christ: nevertheless I live; yet not I, but Christ liveth in me: and the life which I now live in the flesh I live by the faith of the Son of God, who loved me, and gave himself for me." But if the words, "I am crucified with Christ" never have become practical and effective in our lives, then we never will be able to pray in such a way that will enable us to receive. We never will be able to pray powerfully enough for the Lord to hear and answer us.

The Lord is looking for people who persevere in prayer. That doesn't mean we have to pray long prayers during a prayer meeting; we can save those lengthy prayers for when we are at home. Rather, God is looking for people who come before Him in faith in such a way that He can answer immediately.

When we carefully read the Acts of the Apostles, we see that the apostles' prayer meetings produced different results from ours. "And when they had prayed, the place was shaken where they were assembled together; and they were all filled with the Holy Ghost" (Acts 4:31). Does this happen in our prayer meetings? Generally speaking, that is NOT the case. As a result, revival does not occur. It is not the fault of the wicked world or the evil times in which we live; rather, it is the fault of our unbroken selves: "Ye lust, and have not: ye kill, and desire to have, and cannot obtain: ye fight and war." What is the result? "...Ye have not, because ye ask not" (James 4:2). We need to accept Calvary and be crucified with Christ in order to conquer our egos.

2. Resist The Devil

The second thing that must be removed is found in James 4:7: "Submit yourselves therefore to God. Resist the devil, and he will flee from you" (James 4:7). We must begin with ourselves, with our sinful flesh, before we can speak of the outward enemy. Too often we blame the devil when in reality our obstacles are our flesh, our bad character and our sinful nature. This is wrong! Our "self" must first be nailed to the Cross and only then will we be able to recognize the enemy.

Remember, the enemy comes when we have decided to follow the Lord all the way. But the Word of God tells us to resist the devil! In other words, we must resist the demonic influences that surround us. These powers of darkness surround us and whisper blasphemous thoughts into our ears. These are the powers that continually make believers feel dejected or tired when they want to pray.

Don't you face a battle every time you want to go to a prayer meeting? Doesn't it take an extra effort every time you want to pray alone? Isn't there always an excuse — you are overworked, unworthy, sick, tired, have worked so hard or still have so much work to do? There are so many plausible excuses for neglecting prayer.

Are you one who only prays when it is convenient? Faithfulness in prayer is what counts! Satan is behind all these excuses and he wants to keep us from praying. I see how this is true in my own personal life. All hell seems to break loose to keep me from praying. I can do other things such as preach, read, dictate, or counsel, but I am not allowed to pray! However, when we don't pray, we get pulled into the vicious cycle of work, but we accomplish less. If we turn 180 degrees and pray more, the result is that we have more strength and less work.

Suddenly everything begins to run smoothly. Why? This was the secret of Elijah the prophet: "...As the LORD God of Israel liveth, before whom I stand..." (1st Kings 17:1). Elijah did not strive. Based on the facts of his life as detailed in the Bible, we see that he was a man who seldom appeared in public. His work was little in quantity, but mighty in quality. He stands like a pillar in biblical history. It was not without good reason that he appeared with Moses at Jesus'

Transfiguration. Why? Because he was a man of prayer and he possessed authority as a result.

In 1948, I attended Beatenberg Bible School in Switzerland when the first world conference of "Youth for Christ" took place. An elderly man was present among approximately 400 believers. This man belonged to the Gideons. I have forgotten his name, but I will never forget him. I never heard him speak in public, but when I knocked on his door to call him to eat he answered, "I'm sorry, I'm praying." When we passed by his room, we didn't hear a sound. We could almost sense God's holy presence. We saw little of this man, but his personality impressed me because he was a man of prayer.

Do you think something new should begin in your life? Does your life need to be cleansed and purified so that you can resist the enemy? We have no power when our hearts are not cleansed and our egos have not been surrendered in Christ's death.

God's Word admonishes us to "...resist the enemy." The enemy rejoices when our egos are very much alive, or if we are dishonest and do not walk in the truth. But the Bible says, and I repeat, "...resist the devil." Resist the demonic influences from the invisible world. The pathway to prayer opens immediately when we resist the devil. "...Resist the devil, and he will flee from you. Draw nigh to God, and he will draw nigh to you" (James 4:7b–8a). It doesn't say, "Draw near to God, and He will draw near to you" and then "...Resist the devil, and he will flee from you." We must first resist the evil one victoriously in the Name of Jesus; and only then will he flee. Then we will have the power to enter into the inner sanctuary.

3. Go Through The Gates

The third obstacle that must be removed are the stones mentioned in Isaiah 62:10: "Go through, go through the gates." There is no hidden meaning; it's an instruction to simply go through the gates into the sanctuary. But immediately after that, Isaiah adds, "...prepare ye the way of the people." Whoever goes through the gate is preparing the way for the people to come to the Lord! "...cast up, cast up the highway; gather out the stones; lift up a standard for the people." What unspeakable fullness is hidden in this verse!

First, the call to prayer: Go through the gate, the victor's gate into the sanctuary, the Jerusalem above. At the same time, we are to prepare the way for the people. Only a few believers really prepare the way for the people because only a few are able to pray victoriously. If the power of prayer is not present during a prayer meeting, we cannot expect anything to happen. Let's prepare the way for our families, neighbors, friends and co-workers who need to be saved through prayer.

Often we think we've done our job because we've handed someone a tract. Of course, this type of evangelism is necessary, but will it produce any meaningful results if we don't also pray for those receiving the Good News printed in those tracts? The Lord promised us, "Ask and it shall be given unto you." But He also instructed us to, "Prepare ye the way of the people."

Perhaps you are a Christian woman, yet you have become a hindrance to your unbelieving husband because your "religion" speaks louder than your actions. If such is the case, Scripture says, "Gather out the stones."

A German translation of Psalm 84:8 reads as follows: "Blessed is the man whose strength is in thee; in whose heart are the highways to Zion." Is there a highway in your heart that leads to victorious prayer? Or are you stumbling over your "stony" self? If so, gather up the stones of pride, deceit, and impurity. Clear the way so that a highway without obstacles can be formed in your heart!

Don't you think that the Lord wants to lavish His children with His blessings? When we have gone through the gates, prepared the way for the people around us and gathered up the stones, then we will be capable of lifting up a standard for the people. This idea is also found in Isaiah 62: "Lift up a standard for the people." In other words, carry out worldwide missionary work.

4. Break Up Your Fallow Ground

The fourth obstacle is found in the Old Testament book of Hosea: "...break up your fallow ground..."

(Hosea 10:12). The Hebrew translation of this verse says, "Break yourselves betimes fresh ground." Many believers don't want to break up their "fallow ground." In other words, they want to leave things as they are. They allow the stones of offense to remain in their hearts rather than dig them up and bring them into the light. The one who can humbly say, "forgive me" or "I was wrong" is on the right track. Such a person has the power to be reconciled through his humility. We will follow on the highway to Zion when the "stones" of our hearts have been prayerfully removed. Then we will have entered new ground; we are "...breaking up [our] fallow ground."

These four points are so important that it is necessary to summarize for clarity's sake:

1. The flesh must be brought to the Cross, because flesh and blood cannot inherit the kingdom of God.

2. Resist the enemy and he will flee from you. Draw near to God and He will draw near to you.

3. Let there be highways to Zion in your heart.

4. Break up your fallow ground.

May the Lord give you grace to do this now so that He can achieve His goal with and through you so that revival can take place!

Chapter 8

Conditions For Answered Prayer

"...prepare to meet thy God, O Israel"
(Amos 4:12b).

∂●

If we ponder the meaning of the words "prayer for revival," we can sum up the definition with just one phrase: "Meeting the Living God!" A meeting with the Living God through prayer is, in itself, revival; personal revival. The more intense our meetings with the Lord, the more revival will spread.

There are three conditions for a meeting with God:

1. We Must Take Time

We all suffer from a chronic lack of time because our lives are so busy. However, it is always in our best interest to set aside some time in prayer every day, no matter how impossible it may seem.

Did you ever notice how easily we become sidetracked when it is time to go to the Lord in prayer? Whatever seems important at the time is not nearly as important as the time we spend with the Lord!

When a believer prays earnestly and seeks the Lord's face, he may be moved, as if by some invisible power, to say "Amen" as soon as possible so that he can take care of other things. It simply is not our nature to remain in prayer. But let me remind you of the words in Ecclesiastes 8:3: "Be not hasty to go out of his sight." When we really want to approach God, we must put all other matters aside and concentrate on the One who saved our very souls.

Every day, we notice how so many people, including our own selves, waste so much time and energy on trivial things, and fail to take care of the important things. Even more tragic is when we allow such behavior to interfere with our communion with God. We use up all of our energy on nonsensical things and then we are only willing to give God the left-overs. We can only live, serve and preach when we continually meet with the Living God. When we don't do this, we are merely "beating the air" (1st Corinthians 9:26), which is guaranteed to bring us discouragement and sadness because we will be failing to meet with our God.

We wouldn't have room in our churches if we gathered up all those who used to come to our prayer meetings. Many of these people have lost their passion for their first love because they did not have a real and essential meeting with God. If we want to practice victorious prayer, we must take time daily to be still.

Taking time does not mean lying in bed in the morning until we are wide-awake, then quickly reading a few Bible verses before praying. Taking time means waiting before the Lord until we can say, "I have met with the Lord," or rather, "He has met with me." The Lord promised, "...ye shall seek me, and find me, when ye shall search for me with all your heart. And I will be found of you..." (Jeremiah 29:13–14a).

2. Seek Your Place

The second condition for a meeting with God is a consistent location. Of course, you can pray anywhere, but it helps to have a special place designated for your quiet time.

Biblical proof for this suggestion is found in Matthew 6:6. The Lord said, "...when thou prayest, enter into thy closet...." Not in any old place, but "...into thy closet." And then? "...When thou hast shut thy door, pray to thy Father which is in secret." The closed door is very important. It serves to keep others out, and to keep us in! We need to be absolutely alone in order to experience the fact that we are never alone. When we close the door to everything, the Lord will reveal Himself to us. Dinner can wait; the laundry won't go anywhere. Nothing is so pressing that it should prevent us from spending quality time with our Lord in prayer!

An important fact about Jacob is found in Genesis 32:24: "And Jacob was left alone; and there wrestled a man with him." Jacob had always been with his wife, his sons and daughters, his servants and his herds. Everything in his life was always on the go. But when trouble came upon him, he remained alone. The moment he was alone (the moment he closed the door behind him, to put it in New Testament language) a man wrestled with him. There, alone, he had a pivotal meeting with God. Only then could the Lord reveal Himself to him.

It is never too late for a meeting with the Lord. Psalm 103:5 says that He makes everything new: "Who satisfieth thy mouth with good things; so that thy youth is renewed like the eagle's." Such a meeting with the Lord is very precious. It is vital, as we mentioned, to get away from everyone and everything that can draw our attention away from the Lord. That doesn't mean we must lock ourselves in a room and pray for five hours (unless that is how the Lord leads); it simply means that we should get away by ourselves and meet with the Lord.

Two brothers were talking on the telephone. The connection was terrible and one of the brothers finally said, "Close the door of your room and you will be able to hear me." A closed door is necessary when we seek to meet the Lord in prayer.

3. Listen Before You Speak

A third condition for meeting God is to recite Scripture when we pray! We cannot pray victoriously if we have not listened before we speak. We should read God's Word, meditate on it and then go to the Lord in prayer.

Isaiah 55:2–3a says, "Wherefore do ye spend money for that which is not bread? and your labour for that which satisfied not?" In other words, we throw ourselves into our work, but we still are not fulfilled inside. What must we do? The Lord says, "Hearken diligently unto me, and eat ye that which is good, and let your soul delight itself in fatness. Incline your ear, and come unto me: hear, and your soul shall live." We should listen to the Word first, then speak. Time and time again, the words "Speak, Lord, for thy servant heareth," have been spoken and put into practice by various men of God in the Bible. They listened to what the Lord said first: "The Lord GOD hath given me the tongue of the learned, that I should know how to speak a word in season to him that is weary: he wakeneth morning by morning, he wakeneth mine ear to hear as the learned. The Lord GOD hath opened mine ear, and I was not rebellious, neither turned away back" (Isaiah 50:4–5). Not only do we need the tongue of the learned to witness and speak to those who are weary, but we also need it in order to pray with power. We will only have this power when God opens our ears and has been able to speak to us.

The Bible describes a few powerful men of prayer whom the Lord chose. Daniel and Noah were certainly fine examples, and the Lord mentions two more in Jeremiah 15:1: "Then said the LORD unto me, Though Moses and Samuel stood before me, yet my mind could not be toward this people: cast them out of my sight, and let them go forth." Moses and Samuel were extraordinary men of prayer who received many answers to their petitions. Moses learned to listen to God's voice during his 40 years in the wilderness. When he was able to hear God's voice and let God speak to him, then he was able to serve the Lord with power and authority.

As a child, Samuel learned to discern between the Lord's voice and other voices. Children are very receptive to God's voice. What our children see and hear within their families is enormously significant for their future lives.

Samuel was a young boy when he slept in the Temple and learned to discern the Lord's voice from Eli's. In fact, he even had to confront Eli several times after hearing his name called. Finally Eli, the high priest, said to him: "Go, lie down: and it shall be, if he call thee, that thou shalt say, Speak, LORD: for thy servant heareth" (1st Samuel 3:9). The result was all Israel — from Dan to Beersheba — knew that Samuel was a man with whom God spoke.

All of Israel trembled as a result of Moses having listened to the Lord.

These men first listened to God, and then spoke to Him. The Lord spoke with Moses as a man speaks with his friends — face to face. For that reason, he had immense power.

A meeting with the Living God makes us regally independent of the commotion that takes place in our daily lives. We achieve a sublime peace; the peace of God rules our hearts. A meeting with God produces true revival in our hearts and spreads rapidly to others. The more intense this meeting is, the greater the results will be.

Chapter 9

What The Lord Wants To See

"Behold, he prayeth" (Acts 9:11b).

❧

The Lord spoke these words to Ananias when He told him to go to Saul of Tarsus. He also told him exactly where he would find Saul: On the street called Straight. This is where the blind Saul was, of whom the Lord said: "Behold, he prayeth." These explicit words show us how terribly important prayer is to God. With these words, the Lord refutes all the objections raised by Ananias. Paul is proof that prayer changes both people and their ideas. The Lord knew that Ananias and all the believers in Damascus feared Saul. He also knew that Saul was responsible for the death of many, and had even participated in the stoning of Stephen. But He said of him, "Behold, he prayeth."

We must realize that prayer, in and of itself, is paramount because there are all kinds of prayers.

Ananias was amazed that he was given the task of going to Saul of Tarsus because he was praying. He objected: "Lord, I have heard by many of this man, how much evil he hath done to thy saints at Jerusalem: And here he hath authority from the chief priests to bind all that call on thy name" (Acts 9:13–14). In other words: How can You send me to such a man? Ananias was so afraid of Saul that he even contradicted the Lord.

But when the Lord said: "Behold, he prayeth," everything changed. He was actually saying, "Saul is praying in such a way that his prayer has reached me." So we see that effective prayer doesn't depend as much on the fact that we are praying as much as it does on our praying in a way that really reaches God! Only when we pray in this way will our prayers have a mighty effect. Prayer changes everything, but most of all it changes the one who prays.

Saul of Tarsus had been spiritually dead, but his testimony later reveals the way to victorious prayer. When he wrote about himself to the Philippians, he explained why, immediately after his conversion he had prayed in a way that prompted the Lord Himself to action.

Read Paul's testimony carefully: "Though I might also have confidence in the flesh. If any other man thinketh that he hath whereof he might trust in the flesh, I more: Circumcised the eighth day, of the stock of Israel, of the tribe of Benjamin, an Hebrew of the Hebrews; as touching the law, a Pharisee; Concerning zeal, persecuting the church; touching the righteousness which is in the law, blameless" (Philippians 3:4–6). Let's break this passage down to see what clues each phrase offers about Paul before his conversion:

• **"Circumcised the eighth day..."** – Saul had been educated according to religious tradition.

• **"Of the stock of Israel..."** – Saul had a strong sense of national pride.

• **"Of the tribe of Benjamin..."** – Saul enjoyed a tremendous family pride.

• **"An Hebrew of the Hebrews..."** – Saul acknowledged his ancestral pride.

• **"As touching the law, a Pharisee..."** – Saul displayed religious self-righteousness.

• **"Concerning zeal, persecuting the church..."** – Saul meant well and was zealous for God.

• **"Touching the righteousness which is in the law, blameless"** – Saul felt that he "deserved" to find grace in God's eyes. However, in verses 7–8 he says: "But what things were gain to me, those I counted loss for Christ. Yea doubtless, and I count all things but loss for the excellency of the knowledge of Christ Jesus my Lord: for whom I have suffered the loss of all things, and do count them but dung, that I may win

Christ." Three times Paul repeats that he counts all things as "loss" so that he may win Christ. Paul was able to pray powerfully because of this attitude. He was broken in his own being and piety.

I am convinced that at the same moment Paul prayed, thousands and thousands of people all over the world were praying, but the Lord said only of Saul to Ananias: "Behold, he prayeth." Why? Why did He name no other? What was so special about Paul's prayer that God acknowledged it?

A Perfect Heart

Paul's prayer came from the bottom of his heart: "For the eyes of the LORD run to and fro throughout the whole earth, to shew himself strong in the behalf of them whose heart is perfect toward him" (2nd Chronicles 16:9). Quite practically, this means that God's eyes see all praying believers. He looks for those who pray and seek Him with all their hearts: "And ye shall seek me, and find me, when ye shall search for me with all your heart. And I will be found of you, saith the LORD" (Jeremiah 29:13–14a).

A Contrite Spirit

Paul — in contrast to so many believers — could immediately pray so effectively because of his contrite heart. Think of the words of Isaiah 57:15: "For thus saith the high and lofty One that inhabiteth eternity, whose name is Holy; I dwell in the high and holy place, with him also that is of a contrite and humble spirit, to revive the spirit of the humble, and to revive the heart of the contrite ones." Paul was so contrite that the Lord was near him. He only needed to open his mouth to be able to pray in a way that God heard him.

Trembling At His Word

Paul's prayer came from a holy awe, even fear, of the Word of God. Paul knew the Word personally. As a scribe, he had learned it all his life, but now the Word had come from heaven, into his heart: "...Saul, Saul, why persecutest thou me? And he said, Who art thou, Lord? And the Lord said, I am Jesus whom thou persecutest" (Acts 9:4b–5a). Paul was afraid on account of the Lord's Word that had become alive in his heart. He became one of those about whom the Lord spoke through the prophet Isaiah: "For all those things hath mine hand made, and all those things have been, saith the LORD: but to this man will I look, even to him that is poor and of a contrite spirit, and trembleth at my word" (Isaiah 66:2). That is why the Lord could hear Paul's prayer immediately.

In Great Affliction

Saul's prayer was the cry of a man who was in great distress. He was similar to the nation of Israel, to which he belonged in body and soul. The Lord had described Israel's distress to Moses: "...I have surely seen the affliction of my people which are in Egypt, and have heard their cry by reason of their taskmasters; for I know their sorrows; And I am come down to deliver them out of the hand of the Egyptians..." (Exodus 3:7–8a). This scenario also applies to the future. As a people, Israel will be heard of the Lord the moment she cries out to Him. This will happen very soon.

When we consider Israel's future, we find in the origin of this true, effectual prayer in the prophetic words of the Old Testament: "And I will pour upon the house of David, and upon the inhabitants of Jerusalem, the spirit of grace and of supplications: and they shall look upon me whom they have pierced, and they shall mourn for him, as one mourneth for his only son, and shall be in bitterness for him, as one that is in bitterness for his firstborn" (Zechariah 12:10).

What is the origin of this spirit of prayer Saul had? It is not in us, but in God Himself. This is the answer to the question I imagine is in your heart: How can I attain the same attitude of heart as Saul so that the Lord can say of me: "Behold, he prayeth"?

Let's remember that everything comes from above, from the Father of lights, and that includes the spirit of prayer. In Saul, God found a man who fulfilled one important condition: He was willing to receive this spirit of prayer. That's the secret. How do we know? The Lord immediately revealed Saul's rebellious nature: "Saul, Saul, why persecutest thou me...it is hard for thee to kick against the pricks" (Acts 9:4b, 5b). In this, we see the instant and complete subordination of Paul's will to God's will. He prayed: "Lord, what wilt thou have me to do?" (verse 6a). His conversion was so complete and dramatic because he did not merely receive forgiveness of his sins, but he realized that his will now belonged to the Lord. The Lord heard his prayer immediately because Paul surrendered unconditionally.

Chapter 10

Prayer In Times Of Trouble

"And call upon me in the day of trouble: I will deliver
thee, and thou shalt glorify me"
(Psalm 50:15).

❧

Our prayers must be offered to God with all of
our heart. In the midst of prayer, worship and
intercession, this "calling upon the Lord" is
mentioned. Calling upon the Name of the Lord takes
boldness. Only those who are convinced of their own
weakness and inability can call upon the Name of the
Lord. This calling is an expression of total dependence.

Humiliating Trials

Let's take a moment to examine our hearts. When we read the words of Psalm 50:15, are we doing so with an egotistical heart? We must always be mindful that when we experience physical ailments, marriage troubles, parenting challenges, or financial problems, God uses these trials to ground us more deeply in Him. He doesn't use these events to hurt us, but to gently remind us of our dependence upon Him.

Another possibility is that we have brought these events on ourselves, for example, by neglecting our spouses, failing to be consistent in disciplining our children, or by being poor stewards of our finances. But, a humble heart and sincere repentance will restore our communion with the Lord.

Another reason we may experience these difficulties is that they may be God's way of chastening His children. If so, praise the Lord, because Scripture says that He only chastens those whom He loves!

Calling Upon The Lord of Lords

However, we must consider an even deeper spiritual problem. The Spirit of God lays on our heart the fact that we are incapable of changing things ourselves.

We don't have the capability of bringing about a revival; in fact, we are not even able to believe consistently. But that brings us back to one of the conditions I just mentioned: humility. We are completely helpless without the Lord. If we remain mindful of this, we know from the psalmist that when we do call upon the Lord in times of trouble, He promises to deliver us.

Calling upon the Lord is direct and immediate. It doesn't involve calling upon some vague being, but it involves calling "HIM," the Lord of lords! Because this is so direct, He guarantees the answer immediately: "He shall call upon me, and I will answer him: I will be with him in trouble" (Psalm 91:15).

This is tremendous! God is with us when we call upon Him in times of distress. Isn't that comforting news? Quite often we forget that beautiful promise of Scripture.

Mary

Mary was in such a deep despair over the whereabouts of Jesus' body (after He was buried in the tomb), that she didn't even notice the Lord was with her. He is there when we call upon Him during such trouble: "The LORD is nigh unto all them that call upon him..." (Psalm 145:18). Notice that the verse doesn't say that the Lord will come to us eventually, but that He is with us the moment we call upon Him. When the Lord draws close to us in this way, we know that He is answering our prayers. Therefore, it is much better to seek Him than it is to seek the answers to our prayers.

Jabez

Consider Jabez: "And Jabez was more honourable

than his brethren: and his mother called his name Jabez, saying, Because I bare him with sorrow. And Jabez called on the God of Israel, saying, Oh that thou wouldest bless me indeed, and enlarge my coast, and that thine hand might be with me, and that thou wouldest keep me from evil, that it may not grieve me! And God granted him that which he requested" (1st Chronicles 4:9–10).

When we truly understand that He is with us and hears us when we call upon Him, we also will understand why the enemy does everything in his power to convince us that we don't need to call upon the Lord, we can handle it ourselves.

The Enemy Of Faith

When a thief breaks into a house and the homeowner discovers him and cries out, the thief has two options: run out of the house, or stifle the homeowner's cry. In the same manner, when we call upon the Lord in times of distress, the enemy is forced to flee!

Don't be surprised when, after you call upon the Name of the Lord in faith, you experience a great resistance and mighty prayer battle. The enemy will try to stifle your joy in victorious prayer. He comes armed with unbelief, physical ailment, pain, evil thoughts or distractions. He tries everything he can to distract your attention and keep you from calling upon the Name of the Lord.

That is how the enemy tried to work in Jabez. But

a careful look at the text tells us that Jabez resisted the enemy: "…and that thine hand might be with me, and that thou wouldest keep me from evil, that it may not grieve me" (1st Chronicles 4:10). In other words, evil is there, but it doesn't need to grieve us. Subsequently, we read that, "…God granted him that which he requested."

Theoretically, we believe everything the Bible says and we believe that the Lord answers when we call upon Him: "Call unto me, and I will answer thee, and shew thee great and mighty things, which thou knowest not" (Jeremiah 33:3). If that is the case, then why don't we call upon Him more often? Probably because we let ourselves be taken by surprise.

Perhaps you may think, "I'm not capable of shaking off the enemy's distractions!" Of course you are! Because you have an anchor!

Build The Altar

Jacob was weak and miserable, but he called upon the Name of the God of Israel after he had built an altar: "And he erected there an altar, and called it El-elohe-Israel" (God, the God of Israel) (Genesis 33:20). That's the secret!

When we build the altar in our lives, the Cross becomes a reality and we reckon ourselves to be crucified with Christ. That's when we are able to break through. We do not call upon just anybody, but upon the Name of the mighty God of Israel! Calling on the Name of the Lord results in a union of our miserable weakness and His infinite power. However, this promise contains a key that we must use in order to claim it.

Fervent Prayer

We must be in a certain frame of mind when calling upon the Lord: "The effectual fervent prayer of a righteous man availeth much" (James 5:16). That's the key! Take the time to read through the Old Testament book of Hosea, the prophet of love. He speaks very gently when he reveals God's judgment on His people. Hosea was inspired by the Holy Spirit and the Lord lamented several times through him that the people did not call upon Him because they did not know Him: "They are all hot as an oven, and have devoured their judges; all their kings are fallen: there is none among them that calleth unto me" (Hosea 7:7). The people neglected to call upon God because He had become foreign to them.

Further, the Lord lamented: "Hear the word of the LORD, ye children of Israel: for the LORD hath a controversy with the inhabitants of the land, because there is no truth, nor mercy, nor knowledge of God in the land" (Hosea 4:1). In other words, they had so little fellowship with Him that they no longer called upon Him.

How can we call upon someone we do not know, one whose redemptive power we do not experience? The Lord also lamented over a powerless calling upon Him.

Many call upon the Name of the Lord but receive no answer. Why not? "And they have not cried unto me with their heart" (Hosea 7:14). That's the problem!

Let's examine our hearts to see whether we have become lukewarm and indifferent. The Lord wants to reveal Himself and wants to send a revival. He is waiting for those who call upon Him with all their hearts. It is written: "For the eyes of the LORD run to and fro throughout the whole earth, to shew himself strong in the behalf of them whose heart is perfect toward him" (2nd Chronicles 16:9). When we accept this and practice it, the Lord will answer wonderfully!

Chapter 11

What Does It Mean To "Break Through" In Prayer?

"Because I was not cut off before the darkness,
neither hath he covered the darkness from my face"
(Job 23:17).

≈

We may experience darkness within us, and notice that it grows even darker when we pray. But prayer changes everything. We know that we can move the arm of God through prayer. The moment a believer kneels to pray, the powers of unbelief and darkness seize him. Why is that so?

1. Unconfessed Sin

The Lord said: "Therefore if thou bring thy gift to the altar, and there rememberest that thy brother hath ought against thee; Leave there thy gift before the altar, and go thy way; first be reconciled to thy brother, and then come and offer thy gift" (Matthew 5:23–24). We cannot expect the Lord to answer our prayers when we harbor unconfessed sin in our hearts. We are dealing with a holy God. It will become increasingly difficult to approach God when we do not seek Him first for forgiveness.

2. Family Tradition

The hidden, unrecognized sins of parents and grandparents bring curses that often go back three and four generations. Let me explain. We are responsible for our own sins, not those of our parents or grandparents. Traditions are passed on from generation to generation. For example, if parents steal, children will often do likewise. Thus the curse of stealing is upon the children, but each child is nevertheless responsible for his or her own action.

Darkness may come over a person every time he wants to enter the sanctuary through the blood of Jesus. Distracting, often sinful thoughts enter into the mind of a believer when he is about to come before the Lord in prayer. Many believers become so troubled by this that they think they have sinned against the Holy Spirit. Such is not the case. It's not demon possession, but it does involve being surrounded by demonic powers. Many Christians are still oppressed by such inherited dark powers of their parents and grandparents. In this case, it's critical to simply confess this oppression to the Lord, because the Bible says, "Whom the Son shall make free he shall be free indeed." After we seek the Lord's forgiveness, we are able to break through in prayer.

Job

A third type of darkness, one for which we are not responsible, can be explained this way: On one hand, it is Satan's attempt to keep us from praying; on the other, it is allowed by God to form us into prayer warriors.

Satan means for the darkness to cause us to give up, whereas God, in allowing the darkness, uses it to test us to find out to what extent we know Him as the King of kings and Lord of lords.

Job serves as the best illustration of this point. He said: "...when I waited for light, there came darkness" (Job 30:26b). Job sought the Lord with all his heart and the Lord Himself testified that there was none so perfect and upright as he. But this same man was led into such darkness that he lamented: "If I wait, the grave is mine house: I have made my bed in the darkness" (Job 17:13). He was in a desperate situation. But the Lord knew His servant and loved him.

There was so much at stake in Job's trouble. The invisible world looked on and wondered: Will he give up or hold on? Even his own wife tried to persuade him to give up. The Lord's honor was at stake! God expected very much of Job in that He let him go through darkness for a long time and didn't even answer his prayers. But God trusted Job not to sin in spite of this.

If we experience darkness even after we have confessed our sins, we must simply accept this inability to break through the darkness as God's answer to "wait." The devil is waiting for us to give up, but the Lord is also waiting. He is waiting to see if we will hold out, and when we do, we will enjoy a wonderful victory!

Job's attitude was pure; he broke through the darkness and into a mighty prayer victory. Job expressed this in one sentence that has served as a source of strength for millions of people in their hour of death: "I know that my redeemer liveth." If Job had not experienced the darkness, he could have said at the most, "Oh, I believe in God; that's all I can do." But his testimony became all the mightier because it was born out of darkness!

Daniel

Daniel serves as another example. Daniel 10:2–3 contains some very important words: "In those days I Daniel was mourning three full weeks. I ate no pleasant bread, neither came flesh nor wine in my mouth, neither did I anoint myself at all, till three whole weeks were fulfilled."

Why was Daniel so sad? He had recognized from

the Word of God that the seventy years of Israel's exile were coming to an end. "In the first year of his reign I Daniel understood by books the number of the years, whereof the word of the LORD came to Jeremiah the prophet, that he would accomplish seventy years in the desolations of Jerusalem. And I set my face unto the Lord God, to seek by prayer and supplications, with fasting, and sackcloth, and ashes" (Daniel 9:2–3). He was praying in accordance with the Word of God for the salvation of his people — but he received no answer.

Then he decided upon a time of fasting and he prayed for three weeks. During this time he abstained from all comfort.

Although he prayed perseveringly, Daniel was sad because God was silent. But it never occurred to him to give up. That was his greatness.

What if that had been us? What weaklings we are! We might have had a revival long ago if we had not given up in prayer. Praying for revival is in accordance with the will of God.

When God does not answer and permits darkness in our souls, it is only because the victory that follows will be even more glorious.

Finally, Daniel received an answer but first he was given a glimpse of the dark background of his prayer battle. The archangel said to him: "...O Daniel, a man greatly beloved, understand the words that I speak unto thee, and stand upright: for unto thee am I now sent. And when he had spoken this word unto me, I stood trembling. Then he said unto me, Fear not, Daniel: for from the first day that thou didst set thine heart to understand, and to chasten thyself before thy God, thy words were heard, and I am come for thy words. But the prince of the kingdom of Persia withstood me one and twenty days: but lo, Michael, one of the chief princes, came to help me; and I remained there with the kings of Persia" (Daniel 10:11–13). In other words, "Daniel, although you remained in darkness for three weeks, the Lord heard you long ago!"

This also applies when we are praying according to God's will. The Lord has already heard us even though we perceive no visible answer to our prayers. Isn't that wonderful? When we have cried to the Lord for something particular, with the assurance that it is His will, yet we remain in darkness and receive no answer, then we must remember He has heard us from the first moment already. What we have to do is hold out.

Korah

The sons of Korah — in spite of being descendants from a family that had known satanic bondage — could pray mighty prayers of faith. This is exemplified wonderfully in their glorious psalms.

Their ancestors, the whole band of Korah, had gone to hell alive because they rebelled against the Lord. But in one of the psalms of the sons of Korah, we read: "Shall thy wonders be known in the dark?"

(Psalm 88:12). The sons of Korah were redeemed from the curse of their forefathers just as there is complete redemption for all over any and all dark powers because Jesus is the Victor!

David

King David is another example. In spite of his many prayers, he continually experienced the opposite of his petitions during the first years following his anointing to be king. It was as though God was silent; it was as if He had forgotten His word and was ignoring the fact that He Himself had anointed David as king.

So often David lamented: "Lord, I am lying in the pit. Do you not hear my loud cries?" But finally, he came to the overwhelming realization: "Yea, the darkness hideth not from thee; but the night shineth as the day: the darkness and the light are both alike to thee" (Psalm 139:12).

All of us who have to fight against darkness can be comforted by David's words.

Jesus

Our blessed Savior, Jesus Christ, the greatest Man of prayer ever, went through the greatest darkness. From the sixth hour to the ninth hour, darkness fell over the land and Jesus cried aloud: "My God, my God, why hast thou forsaken me?" (Matthew 27:45–46). He received no answer to this question, but God's silence led to the most glorious victory of all times, a victory that is valid in eternity.

Woe unto us if we are so unbelieving that we give up when we encounter times of darkness and resistance. We throw everything away when we stop praying even though the victory is imminent. Therefore, keep on praying despite all negative feelings. Remember the words of Isaiah 50:10: "Who is among you that feareth the LORD, that obeyeth the voice of his servant, that walketh in darkness, and hath no light? let him trust in the name of the LORD, and stay upon his God." Jesus lives!

Chapter 12

When God Is Silenced

"And it shall come to pass, that before they call,
I will answer..." (Isaiah 65:24).

"I called him, but he gave me no answer"
(Song of Solomon 5:6).

❧

At first glance, these two verses appear to be contradictory in nature; therefore, an explanation is necessary. Our own personal lives attest to the fact that both verses of Scripture are true. At times, the Lord has intervened even before we have offered up our prayers: "...before they call, I will answer."

Perhaps you have experienced various troubles in your life. You may have wondered how to cope with a situation, but then, when you were confronted with the problem, it seemed to have disappeared.

The women who came to Jesus' grave faced a problem: "And very early in the morning the first day of the week, they came unto the sepulchre at the rising of the sun. And they said among themselves, Who shall roll us away the stone from the door of the sepulchre? And when they looked, they saw that the stone was rolled away: for it was very great" (Mark 16:2–4). These women went to the tomb in search of Jesus' body, but the tomb was empty! The Lord was alive, only they didn't know it yet.

Their problem was that they knew they weren't strong enough to roll away the heavy stone. They went to the tomb with this great burden in their hearts. Yet even as they were troubled over it, the object of their worry already had disappeared. They experienced the promise: "...before they call, I will answer."

We can be burdened with all sorts of cares and problems, but as soon as we take the time to pour out our hearts before the Lord in faith and identify our troubles to Him, we will notice that in the midst of prayer, our burdens are suddenly rolled onto God. This is the practical application of the words, "Casting all your care upon him, for he careth for you" (1st Peter 5:7). We hardly have time to thank Him before He performs another miracle in our lives. When the Lord hears our prayers, He answers them thoroughly, and in such a way that we can hardly believe it. This is clearly written in Paul's letter to the Ephesians. "Now unto him that is able to do exceeding abundantly above all that we ask or think, according to the power that worketh in us" (Ephesians 3:20).

When God Doesn't Answer

But what happens when God is silent and doesn't appear to answer? God's silence can have various meanings. Often, His silence is the most profound answer we can receive from Him.

Recently someone told me that he did not feel the Lord's presence. He was desperately striving to abide in Jesus, yet he felt that the Lord was far away. My advice was to thank God, cling to His promises, and build upon the rock of faith even if he did not "feel" anything.

God's Word remains the same at all times. Our feelings fluctuate a million times a day! We glorify the Lord most when we take Him at His word, even when He may seem far away and does not answer our prayers. This is putting Isaiah 50:10 into practice: "Who is among you that feareth the LORD, that obeyeth the voice of his servant, that walketh in darkness, and hath no light? let him trust in the name of the LORD, and stay upon his God." Glorify the Lord when darkness surrounds you and you are feeling oppressed.

Two major reasons that God doesn't seem to answer, or that His answers seem delayed or even limited, are outlined below:

1. An Interrupted Relationship With The Lord

Many people who come to me for counseling tell me that they claim the Scripture: "Ask and ye shall receive...and all things, whatsoever ye shall ask in prayer, believing, ye shall receive." They say that God simply does not answer. That may be true, but it's only half true. If God doesn't answer because of an interruption in our relationship with Him, then the reason lies with the one who lodged the complaint. In such a case, God's silence corresponds to what the Lord said concerning Israel in Isaiah 1:15: "And when ye spread forth your hands, I will hide mine eyes from you: yea, when ye make many prayers, I will not hear: your hands are full of blood." Or, "Behold, the LORD's hand is not shortened, that it cannot save; neither his ear heavy, that it cannot hear: But your iniquities have separated between you and your God, and your sins have hid his face from you, that he will not hear. For your hands are defiled with blood, and your fingers with iniquity; your lips have spoken lies, your tongue hath muttered perverseness" (Isaiah 59:1–3). Our disobedience may be the reason for God's silence; it may have interrupted our contact with the Lord. We must consistently search our hearts and confess our sins to the Lord so that when we approach Him in prayer, we will be found pleasing to Him.

This fact is also found in Psalm 66:18: "If I regard iniquity in my heart, the Lord will not hear me." Sin interrupts our fellowship with God. This should not come as a surprise. Surprising, however, is that we usually do forget this fact, and are no longer shocked by it. Our consciences have become insensitive, and we disregard this divine principle.

We could put it this way: Prayer is how we commune with God; however, sin disrupts it. God is holy, pure and without sin. When we, who are fallen, allow sin in our lives, it is a slap in His face. How can we expect to speak with God when our lives do not reflect a heart of obedience to Him? Prayer is basically cooperation with the eternal God; therefore, a clear unobstructed relationship with Him is necessary. Scripture says that we are laborers together with God; therefore, we must examine our relationship with Him.

2. Interrupted By Sin

We can easily establish contact with the enemy through participation in activities the Lord does not want us to do. There may be sin that others feel comfortable with, but we do not. The Master wants us to abstain from that activity.

When we do sin and recognize it, it should

absolutely devastate us, because we have sinned against the Lord who saved us from darkness. The quiet voice of the Holy Spirit who convicts us of sin is ignored when we choose to sin. By ignoring this conviction, we interrupt our relationship with the Lord and side with the enemy. As a result, our prayer life is paralyzed.

Shall we go to the Lord in prayer and ask: "Dear Father in heaven, why has my relationship with You been interrupted?" Satan rejoices when we show weakness in our prayers. The most serious consequence of a weak prayer life is that it hinders lost souls from being saved and revival is delayed. Let's be careful to maintain our fellowship with the Living God through Jesus Christ.

Chapter 13

Resistance Against Prayer

"In those days I Daniel was mourning three full weeks. I ate no pleasant bread, neither came flesh nor wine in my mouth, neither did I anoint myself at all, till three whole weeks were fulfilled...Then I lifted up mine eyes, and looked, and behold, a certain man clothed in linen...And he said unto me...Fear not, Daniel: for from the first day that thou didst set thine heart to understand, and to chasten thyself before thy God, thy words were heard, and I am come for thy words. But the prince of the kingdom of Persia withstood me one and twenty days: but, lo, Michael, one of the chief princes, came to help me; and I remained there with the kings of Persia. Now I am come to make thee understand what shall befall thy people in the latter days..." (Daniel 10:2–3,5,11,12–14a).

❧

We must take another look at God's beloved servant Daniel. Resistance began the moment he earnestly sought the Lord in prayer. The prince of the kingdom of Persia personified the outward resistance from the invisible world. We must never forget that a battle begins when we pray and draw near to God with a true heart, having our evil conscience sprinkled by the blood of Christ as it says in Hebrews 10:22. Now we must stand against the dark world of demons.

Daniel prayed to the Lord for twenty-one days, but God didn't answer until the last day. The angel who came to him assured him: "...from the first day that thou didst set thine heart to understand, and to chasten thyself before thy God, thy words were heard, and I am come for thy words" (verse 12). He confirmed that Daniel's heart attitude was correct because he truly wanted to find the Lord, who promised: "And ye shall seek me, and find me, when ye shall search for me with all your heart. And I will be found of you, saith the LORD" (Jeremiah 29:13–14a). But the answer didn't come immediately; it required a great deal of perseverance on Daniel's part.

When we lift up our hearts to God in Jesus' Name,

we have already been heard; that is, the answer is on its way, even if we do not see it yet.

Resistance From The Invisible World

Notice the expression, "...from the first day that thou didst set thine heart...." Here we are confronted with resistance in the invisible world. Satan knows very well that those who persevere in prayer are invincible. Only the enemy's stubborn resistance and God's silence teach us that the answer is already there: "Before they call, I will answer." Only spiritually minded people such as Daniel who are not bound by worldly things can grasp this: "In those days I Daniel was mourning three full weeks. I ate no pleasant bread, neither came flesh nor wine in my mouth, neither did I anoint myself at all..." (verse 2).

Resistance From The Visible World

Another type of resistance we must address is from the visible world. This becomes very real when we pray victoriously. Whether we pray alone or in a prayer meeting, the enemy uses our environment to distract and prevent us from breaking through to the Lord in prayer.

The enemy offers us an alibi so that we can say, "I'll pray later." But we all know "later" never comes. Only prayer warriors are capable of turning the short time we have into an eternally valuable commodity. We will be victorious when we stop listening to the enemy who tries to convince us that we have neither the time nor the strength to pray.

I am certain that you will agree that many times in your life as a believer, something always comes up when you get on your knees to pray. We show our weakness when we decide that sleep is more important than communion with God. If such is the case, consider changing the pattern of your prayer life. Pray in the morning, throughout the day, or in your car — but avoid praying at the end of the day when the temptation to go to sleep is so strong.

Our entire fellowship and reliance on God is demonstrated through prayer. Apart from the Lord we can do nothing. He didn't save us only to say, "You're on your own now." He is with us always. He expects our best because He gave us His best and continues to do so every minute of our lives!

Resistance Of Prayer Within Us

Our inner nature is vitally important if we expect to pray victoriously. By nature we are lazy when it comes to praying. The frightful thing is that the father of lies always gives us a reason for our laziness. If only believers realized the real reason for their laziness in prayer!

Laziness

The Bible also shows us another aspect responsible for our laziness: "Wherefore seeing we also are compassed about with so great a cloud of witnesses, let us lay aside every weight, and the sin which doth so easily beset us..." (Hebrews 12:1). Who are these witnesses? They are those who have died in the Lord. Do our deceased brethren share our lives on earth? No. They do not share the joy and pain that take place in our daily lives, but they do share in our victories. Every victory of faith we experience on this earth is registered in heaven. Those departed believers have overcome; therefore, they register the victories in our lives. They are the "...great...cloud of witnesses." We must never pray for those who are in heaven; that is spiritism. But those who are asleep in the Lord belong to the cloud of witnesses who see whether or not we overcome.

Let's carefully read Hebrews 12:1 again: "Wherefore seeing we also are compassed about with so great a cloud of witnesses, let us lay aside every weight, and the sin which doth so easily beset us." The Revised Bible and many other translations render this last phrase, "...the sin which doth closely cling to us."

I'm not going to get into particular sins because I believe Scripture speaks of sin in general in this context. What is "...the sin which doth so easily beset us"? In Psalm 119:25, David said, "My soul cleaveth unto the dust: quicken thou me according to thy word." In other words, we are made of flesh and blood and everything in us is sinful. Paul confessed: "I know that in me (that is, in my flesh,) dwelleth no good thing."

Our spirits become new when we are born again.

The new spirit is blameless, righteous, holy and sinless. But the flesh is sin. For this reason, the apostle admonishes us to lay sin aside so that we can pray.

Our natural man is very cunning and will always come up with excuses. Our flesh is not capable of lifting itself up to God, but is subject to the law of sin and death.

It's the same with the law of gravity. Place any object in your hand, and it will not remain suspended in the air without the support of a hand. Because it cannot think or feel, it becomes subject to the law of gravity. It will always fall when released. This is how we are subject to the law of sin and death in our nature of flesh and blood. We are continually being dragged down. What does the Word of God say? We are to lay aside everything that drags us down! Where are we to lay it? At the Cross of Calvary! Here we return to the point we emphasized in Chapter Three: We must be crucified with Christ.

The Loss Of Our First Love

A further type of inner resistance to prayer arises through the loss of our first love. We can only pray victoriously, and from the depths of our hearts, when the Lord is our first love. If this is not the case, we are just going through the motions. When a prayer meeting becomes nothing more than an opportunity to socialize, it loses its importance as corporate intercession. Then there really is no point in going on. Several people in the church who may only be there because they feel it is the "right" thing to do. Their hearts may not be in it, their sincerity may easily be challenged, and they can ruin the beauty of the Body coming together to pray to their God. Yes, there may be times when we drag ourselves home from the office, choke down our dinner and grudgingly get back in the car and head for the church. But haven't you also noticed that, many of those times, we receive a blessing in a special way? Those occasions turn out to be a sweet time of fellowship with the Lord. God rewards our efforts and diligence by giving us a special time of fellowship with Him.

When we allow ourselves to be led back to our first love through repentance, our inner attitude will be such that we can hardly wait to go to the next prayer meeting.

Prayer and revival are like cause and effect. What will the effect be if the cause is not clear and the prayer is not coming from a pure heart? If such is the case, we have no right to question why revival has not taken place. True revival must first take place in the heart of every individual believer. It's got to come from the believer first, and then it will spread out into the unbelieving world.

If the Lord Jesus is saying to you, "I have somewhat against thee, because thou hast left thy first love," then you must repent and ask the Lord to be your first love again so that you can come to Him with a cleansed heart.

Chapter 14

Prayer In The Name Of Jesus

"Verily, verily, I say unto you, Whatsoever ye shall ask the Father in my name, he will give it you. Hitherto have ye asked nothing in my name: ask, and ye shall receive, that your joy may be full" (John 16:23b–24).

"Whatsoever ye shall ask of the Father in my name, he may give it you" (John 15:16b).

✥

The words "verily, verily," are always followed by some great spiritual truth. For example: "Verily, verily, I say unto thee, Except a man be born again, he cannot see the kingdom of God"

(John 3:3). To Peter He said, "Verily, verily, I say unto thee, When thou wast young, thou girdedst thyself, and walkedst whither thou wouldest: but when thou shalt be old, thou shalt stretch forth thy hands, and another shall gird thee, and carry thee whither thou wouldest not" (John 21:18).

In Jesus' Name

Here the Lord is giving us another important spiritual truth: When we draw near to the Father, we must never forget to pray in Jesus' Name. But that doesn't always mean that God will answer.

Let's take a few moments to discuss what it means to pray in Jesus' Name. When we pray to the Father in Jesus' Name, this means nothing more than accepting His walk, His way, His nature, His goal and His requests. This is immensely important.

Walk As He Walked

When we become followers of the Lord, we are expected to walk in the way that Jesus walked: "He that saith he abideth in him ought himself also so to walk, even as he walked" (1st John 2:6). His walk was an expression of His faith. He endured as seeing Him who is invisible.

It is not only a matter of having the same walk, but also the same way. Whoever prays in Jesus' Name is a hypocrite and a liar if he is not willing to go exactly the same way Jesus went.

Follow His Way

Revelation 14:4 says, "...which follow the Lamb whithersoever he goeth." To go the same way is even more definite than walking as He walked. What does this way look like? Scripture says that the way is narrow and the gate is straight. In other words, the narrow way offers many possible deviations. It is very easy to leave the narrow way, but the Lamb is leading the way; we are not following the narrow way, but we are following the Lamb. The way the Lamb leads was paved through His death.

According to Hebrews 10:19, it is the only way to holiness: "Having therefore, brethren, boldness to enter into the holiest by the blood of Jesus." It becomes apparent, especially in prayer, just how far we have progressed along this way. Inner unity with the Lamb enables us to advance. This is immediately noticeable when people pray. We will be accepted at the Lord's throne when we follow in Jesus' footsteps.

The Way Of The Lamb

The condition for prayer in Jesus' Name is not only an acceptance of His walk and His way, but it is also an identification with His nature. The Lamb was obedient unto death, yet we find it so easy to rebel and say, "I've had enough!"

When we read Hebrews 5:8–9, we see how the Lord Jesus Christ learned obedience as a young man: "Though he were a Son, yet learned he obedience by the things which he suffered; And being made perfect, he became the author of eternal salvation unto all them that obey him." How did Jesus learn obedience? Through suffering! He was not a shouter; He was silent. A true person of prayer does not talk a lot nor does he gossip. The Lamb was silent in suffering. The more we speak about our suffering, and the less we are still, the farther we stray from the narrow way of following Jesus. The nature of the Lamb decides our prayer life.

In this connection, let's also read 1st Peter 2:21–25: "For even hereunto were ye called: because Christ also suffered for us, leaving us an example, that ye should follow his steps: Who did no sin, neither was guile found in his mouth: Who, when he was reviled, reviled not again; when he suffered, he threatened not; but committed himself to him that judgeth righteously: Who his own self bare our sins in his own body on the tree, that we, being dead to sins, should live unto righteousness: by whose stripes ye were healed. For ye were as sheep going astray; but are now returned unto the Shepherd and Bishop of your souls."

The Way Of Humility

The way of the Lamb is paved, and it is also a humble way. Humility was not merely one of the Lord's virtues, but it is the basic characteristic of His nature. For this reason, He said: "...I am meek and lowly in heart" (Matthew 11:29). Humility is an expression of the extinguished self. The Lord was neither hard, nor sentimental, nor emotional. He was not proud, nor did He have an inferiority complex.

You may be thinking, "But I'm not like Jesus. I don't have this nature; therefore, I can't pray like that." I would like to show you a biblical example that should serve as an encouragement.

In his youth, Moses was a very hot-tempered man, but when he was old we read: "Now the man Moses was very meek, above all the men which were upon the face of the earth" (Numbers 12:3). That is why Moses had such a big heart and the capacity to bear the burden of others. That is why his power to be silent reflected his power to pray. He was able to be silent before God for forty days and forty nights. The result was that he became meek.

We may be harassed by outward influences that seek to revive our egos. But if we allow ourselves to get caught up in these influences, we lose the mind of Christ and subsequently; we also lose the power to pray.

The Goal Is The Father

To pray in Jesus' Name means to have the same goal He had. What goal did the Lord have? This is expressed in His prayer, "Touch me not; for I am not yet ascended to my Father: but go to my brethren, and say unto them, I ascend unto my Father, and your Father; and to my God, and your God" (John 20:17). With these words, Jesus was communicating that we both have the same goal: Our Father in heaven!

Glorify God

Now we come to the closest connection. It is having the same ultimate prayer requests as Jesus. Jesus' priority was always to glorify His Father! When the disciples asked Him: "Lord, teach us to pray..." (Luke 11:1), He revealed the greatest prayer request: "Our Father which art in heaven, Hallowed be thy name. Thy kingdom come. Thy will be done..." In other words, "Not I, but You; not my will, but thine." If we constantly come to the Lord with our hands open, waiting for Him to give us something, we immediately lose sight of the meaning and value of prayer. We are called to glorify God with our thoughts, our prayers and our lives.

Does the Lord start speaking about Himself or His disciples in His high-priestly prayer? No. It is all about His Father: "These words spake Jesus, and lifted up his eyes to heaven, and said, Father, the hour is come; glorify thy Son, that thy Son also may glorify thee: As thou hast given him power over all flesh..." (John 17:1–2). The only intention of His prayer was to glorify His Father, not Himself or His environment.

God's actions do not concentrate on the nations, but on the little city of Jerusalem in which the Lord revealed Himself historically and in which He will reveal Himself in the future. Of the nations we read: "Behold, the nations are as a drop of a bucket, and are counted as the small dust of the balance..." (Isaiah 40:15). The nations are mentioned in one short sentence while we find whole chapters dedicated to the city of the great King.

When God alone is our goal, our lives will be full of the glory of heaven. When we want to be more like Jesus, we will also be able to pray as He did. We will pray more, for never did a man pray so much as the One who spent whole nights in prayer before God.

Chapter 15

Prayer Out Of A Knowledge Of God

"After this manner therefore pray ye: Our Father which art in heaven, Hallowed by thy name. Thy kingdom come. Thy will be done in earth, as it is in heaven" (Matthew 6:9–10).

୨෧

The will of God is to be realized through prayer. Jesus said, "Thy will be done in earth, as it is in heaven." In other words, our requests do not come first; our first priority should be giving God the glory due Him.

Some may suggest that this contradicts what Jesus

said in John 15:7: "If ye abide in me, and my words abide in you, ye shall ask WHAT YE WILL, and it shall be done unto you." This passage says nothing about praying for God's will, but the exact opposite. How is God's holy will to be united with our own? If we are absolutely honest, we must admit that, by nature, we always tend to desire our way, not God's. Whoever has not recognized that yet does not know himself. We are so self-centered in our prayer lives that we often think that all of our requests are according to God's will, when in fact they often originate from our own will.

Abiding In Jesus

"Thy will be done in earth, as it is in heaven." "If ye abide in me, and my words abide in you, ye shall ask what ye will, and it shall be done unto you"? Is there a key to understanding these seemingly contradictory statements Jesus made? Yes. The key to this promise is a condition Jesus named: "If ye abide in me, and my words abide in you."

To abide in Jesus does not require effort; it merely requires us to allow ourselves to fall into His strong arms.

Christ Lives In Us By Faith

According to John 15:14, there are two aspects of abiding in Jesus: "Abide in me, and I in you...." Remember, when the Lord made this statement He was no longer physically on earth, but He was in His

154

glorified body seated at the right hand of the Father. At the same time, He lives in our hearts through the Holy Spirit: "That Christ may dwell in your hearts by faith..." (Ephesians 3:17a).

It was just the opposite before the Lord went to the Cross: His spirit was with the Father when He physically walked the earth. John 3:13 says: "And no man hath ascended up to heaven, but he that came down from heaven, even the Son of man which is in heaven."

Then He went to the Cross and died for our sins, was buried, rose on the third day and finally ascended into heaven, where He now sits at the right hand of God (Ephesians 1:20). From this seat in heaven, He exercises all power and authority not only in this world, but also in the world to come. Therefore, His position is one of uncontested victory. Yet at the same time He lives in our hearts by faith!

We Are In Heaven

Where are we when the Lord says: "Abide in me, and I in you"? We are here on earth in our sinful, mortal bodies, but our regenerate spirits are in heaven: "For our conversation is in heaven..." (Philippians 3:20). It doesn't say that our conversation will be in heaven, but that it is already in heaven.

Ephesians 2:6 says: "...And hath raised us up together, and made us sit together in heavenly places in Christ Jesus." While we remain on this earth, our spirits are in Jesus Christ. When the Lord said,

155

"Abide in me, and I in you," He meant that He wants us to abide with Him in this uncontested, victorious position risen with Him and seated with Him in heavenly places.

The words, "...and I in you," remind us to give Him complete dominion over our hearts through the Holy Spirit. That way we are in continual spiritual contact with Him. That's how we can ask what "...we will..." because our wills are synchronized with the holy will of God.

When we form an organic unity with the Lord, we attain a knowledge of the Father such as Jesus had. His strength becomes our strength; His victory, our victory; His love, our love; His patience, our patience; and His willingness to suffer also becomes ours. We also receive unsurpassing knowledge of the Father.

He Is Our Father

In order to pray victoriously, we must know HIM to whom we pray! For this reason, the Lord Jesus said: "After this manner therefore pray ye: Our Father..." (Matthew 6:9). "Our Father" expresses a deep, intimate union with the Lord. Our prayers become quite different when we have knowledge of the Father. They become defined and they are an expression of a full-fledged assurance of faith.

When we pray with the knowledge and assurance of who God is, we can be sure that He hears us. We also know, as we mentioned before, that He has already heard our prayer.

Is this an over-statement? No! We find biblical support of this fact in Matthew 6. This is very important, especially for those who feel they must pray eloquent prayers in order to make a good impression. Such prayers are not victorious ones. The Lord said: "But when ye pray, use not vain repetitions, as the heathen do: for they think that they shall be heard for their much speaking. Be not ye therefore like unto them: for your Father knoweth what things ye have need of, before ye ask him" (Matthew 6:7–8). Our logic argues that in such a case, we don't have to pray at all. Oh yes we do! Such prayer in faith prepares us for God's blessing to flow through us.

We Must Know The Father

That's what it means to have the knowledge of the Father, as Jesus had. John 11:41 says: "And Jesus lifted up his eyes, and said, Father, I thank thee that thou HAST heard me." Lazarus had been lying in a tomb for four days when Jesus offered this prayer to God. However, the Lord had such knowledge of the Father that He never doubted, even though He knew Lazarus was dead: "...I thank thee that thou HAST heard me." This is the kind of prayer that conquers everything.

Knowledge of the Father helps us to pray specifically and gives us an inner assurance that no one can take from us. We do not let ourselves be influenced by what we see, but only by what God has prepared for us in His glory.

Moreover, when we pray in the knowledge of God, we will also be able to pray in faith. Then we will also be able to understand Jesus' demand: "Be ye therefore perfect, even as your Father which is in heaven is perfect" (Matthew 5:48).

Perfect In Him

This is an impossible demand for our human understanding. How can we be perfect as God is perfect? Let's look to Jesus for our answer. Jesus had such authority in prayer because He knew the Father. How did He know the Father so well? Because He was one with His Father!

You may say, "Of course the Lord Jesus was one with His Father from eternity." That is true, and for this very reason He came, in order to — as Paul put it — "lead us back to God," which we read in Colossians 3:3: "...your life is hid with Christ in God." For what purpose? So that we become true followers in Christ.

The Father's Eternal Faithfulness

The Lord describes His love for Zion in such a moving manner: "Can a woman forget her sucking child, that she should not have compassion on the son of her womb? yea, they may forget, yet will I not forget thee. Behold, I have graven thee upon the palms of my hands" (Isaiah 49:15–16a). That is motherly love! And in Psalm 89:26 we may say with David, "Thou art my father." This is the loving Father. The more intimately we know the Lord, the more we will resemble Him in His nature and become "fathers" and "mothers" in Christ. Then our struggle with prayer will end and we will be able to pray without ceasing.

When we have continual contact with the Lord, we will also have His nature. A sublime sense of peace will wash over us so that we will be able to say: "Father, I thank thee that thou hast heard me." Then we will know the power of spiritual fatherhood.

The Apostle John shows us the four stages of being a child of God: little children, children, young men and fathers. We will briefly discuss each stage now.

Little Children

Babies and toddlers require a great deal of work. A baby's needs must be tended before anyone else's. John wrote about these little children in his first letter: "I write unto you, little children, because your sins are forgiven you for his names' sake" (1st John 2:12). Taking care of a baby involves the daily repetition of feeding him, changing his diaper, and putting him to bed. Eating and sleeping are the baby's only desire; nothing else seems to matter.

It is similar with babies in Christ. Their most important need is for their sins to be forgiven. They cannot pray: they only cry. They cannot say "Abba, Father," because they have not yet learned to say these words, nor to distinguish their father. Their moods are subject to their circumstances. They can

159

seem inconsolable one moment and happy the next. "Baby" Christians can be deeply offended one day, and alright the next. These "babies" need the same amount of attention as a literal baby. They need to be discipled by a more seasoned Christian. They need to have the Word of God spoon-fed to them. They can crawl and may even be able to take small steps, but since they are so new in the faith, they must go slowly. Their newfound love for the Lord leaves them frustrated because they want to run and dive into the Word, but instead, they trip over their own two feet. It is a wonderful thing when a baby Christian is born; however, it's a tragedy when he remains stunted in his growth.

Young Children

John wrote about young children in verse 13: "I write unto you, little children, because ye have known the Father." The Amplified Version of the Bible refers to these children as "boys" or "lads." The difference between a baby and a child is that a child now knows his parents more intimately. Whereas a baby simply depends on those two people he sees every day to take care of his basic needs, a child must be treated differently. A child can do more to take care of himself, but he still requires parental guidance.

Young Men

John mentioned the third stage (young men) twice because it is very important to the Church of Jesus

Christ. The "young men" stage is written about in 1st John 2:13b and 14b: "I write unto you, young men, because ye have overcome the wicked one...I have written unto you, young men, because ye are strong, and the word of God abideth in you, and ye have overcome the wicked one." Who are the spiritual young men in the Church? They are the men and women, girls and boys who have tasted victory in Jesus. They have experienced answer to prayer. This is quite a jump from being a child, isn't it?

Generally speaking, the Church of Jesus Christ is made up of believers from two groups: the majority includes "babies," while a smaller portion includes "young men." Unfortunately, in many cases, the babies remain babies. They enjoy being spoon-fed and lack the motivation to dig deeper into God's Word because they feel it requires too much work.

A young man, although his position in Christ has matured, cannot remain a young man in Christ. He must grow.

In John 15, Jesus said that God purges the branches that do not bear fruit. In other words, if you have been in Christ for 20 years yet you have never met with the Lord in prayer, studied His Word, or told others of Him, you run the risk of being removed from the Vine. That means you will not bear fruit for the glory of His Name.

Salvation is not a mental assent; it is a growing, maturing relationship with God. It is not a one-time, "Yes, I believe." It is a process that develops as it is nurtured.

Fathers

"I write unto you, fathers, because ye have known him that is from the beginning" (1st John 2:13a).

We are to grow in the knowledge of the Father, which leads to spiritual fatherhood and motherhood. These are seasoned Christians. Before they do anything, they meet with the Lord in prayer. Spiritual "fathers" and "mothers" are consumed with the Lord, whom they know they ultimately will meet face to face. They seek the Lord before they begin their days. They meditate on His Word day and night. They are grieved if they miss worship, fellowship and prayer. Their lives revolve wholly around the Lord, who saved their lives!

On a personal note: Let's always be mindful to evaluate our position in Christ. Of the four categories we just named, which one most accurately describes you?

Prayer Warriors

Our final section in this chapter has to do with prayer warriors. Remember Amalek's attack on Israel in Exodus 17? Joshua was leading Israel in battle, but his victory depended on the prayers of Moses, a spiritual father who did nothing but pray. "And it came to pass, when Moses held up his hand, that Israel prevailed: and when he let down his hand, Amalek prevailed" (Exodus 17:11). Do you see how important it is to pray? Unfortunately, our arms become tired too quickly.

The most important thing for us to do is to persevere in prayer in the knowledge of God. When we don't know the Lord intimately, we waste much energy in prayer, and it becomes a struggle. But knowledge of the Lord produces spiritual fertility.

Abraham

Abraham, who is called "father" seven times in Romans 4, had great authority! What did he say to the king of Sodom? "I have lift up mine hand unto the LORD, the most high God, the possessor of heaven and earth, That I will not take from a thread even to a shoelatchet, and that I will not take any thing that is thine, lest thou shouldest say, I have made Abram rich" (Genesis 14:22–23). This was his power. He knew the nature of God.

Elijah

What about Elijah? Every time I'm on Mount Carmel, I think of the critical moment when Elijah — surrounded by thousands and thousands of Israelites and the priests of Baal — prayed a very short prayer: "LORD God of Abraham, Isaac, and of Israel, let it be known this day that thou art God in Israel, and that I am thy servant, and that I have done all these things at thy word. Hear me, O LORD, hear me, that this people may know that thou art the LORD God..." (1st Kings 18:36–37). Elijah must have been very confident! How he would have been put to shame if God had not answered! Elijah had such a knowledge of the Father that he was one with the Father; therefore, he did not doubt for a second that the Lord would answer.

When he was taken up to heaven, Elisha called after him: "My father, my father" (2nd Kings 2:12).

Paul

Think of Paul, who reprimanded the Corinthians and corrected them almost ironically on account of the accusations brought against him. But then, in a tender and fatherly manner, he said, "I write not these things to shame you, but as my beloved sons I warn you...for in Christ Jesus I have begotten you through the gospel" (1st Corinthians 4:14, 15b).

Believers grow in the knowledge of God. Through this knowledge they receive spiritual authority, become mightier in prayer, and persevere until the Lord answers. They pray with the assurance that He has already heard, and they wait patiently for the answer to become visible.

Chapter 16

The Importance Of Giving Thanks

"…Mattaniah, which was over the thanksgiving, he and his brethren" (Nehemiah 12:8b).

᷾

Here we see the only expression of the office of thanksgiving mentioned in the entire Bible. Of the men who returned from Babylon and Persia, Nehemiah appointed one to be in charge of the thanksgiving.

We know that giving thanks is an expression of faith, but are we aware of how the Lord waits for our thanks? The Lord reacts immediately, visibly, and mightily when we thank Him with all our heart. Giving thanks shows God that we believe.

Lamenting and complaining — including our complaining about having too much to do — amounts to nothing more than sheer unbelief because we have a source of strength which never fails.

I want to reemphasize that the Lord reacts to thanks immediately. When we thank God for how He has blessed us, or for how He has given us grace to triumph through a necessary trial, the power of the enemy is broken.

Jehoshaphat

Second Chronicles 20 serves as a good example of this point. King Jehoshaphat was forced to confess his fear to the Lord when the Ammonites and Moabites came to fight against him.

He was told: "There cometh a great multitude against thee from beyond the sea on this side Syria" (verse 2). It would appear that this man did not have great faith, but herein lies the secret of faith; namely, that we tell the Lord the truth rather than sugar coat our sinful ugliness. He knows us inside and out, so there is absolutely no reason to hide our fears, weaknesses and shortcomings from Him.

Jehoshaphat confessed that he was powerless: "O our God, wilt thou not judge them? for we have no might against this great company that cometh against us" (verse 12).

He also confessed that he was helpless: "...neither

know we what to do..." (verse 12b).

What can the Lord do with people who confess they are powerless and helpless? Jehoshaphat learned that in such a situation, he must pray to the Lord, for he said: "...but our eyes are upon thee" (verse 12b). He managed to break through to the Lord in prayer and cast the burden of the impending threat of the Moabite and Ammonite armies upon the Lord so that he could proclaim: "Believe in the LORD your God, so shall ye be established..." (verse 20b).

Jehoshaphat's faith was so infectious that his actions led all the people to express their faith. This was a true revival! Israel no longer trembled at the sight of this threatening army, but they believed in the invisible Lord.

The victorious faith of this people is expressed in verse 22: "And when they began to sing and to praise, the LORD set ambushments against the children of Ammon, Moab, and mount Seir, which were come against Judah; and they were smitten."

All Israel had to do was watch how the Lord intervened. The enemies ended up destroying themselves. "For the children of Ammon and Moab stood up against the inhabitants of mount Seir, utterly to slay and destroy them: and when they had made an end of the inhabitants of Seir, every one helped to destroy another" (verse 23). All that remained was for Israel to give thanks to the Lord! The enemy may threaten, oppress and torment us; however, he is beaten when we pray our way through to thanksgiving. Let us give thanks until revival comes!

Offering Thanks Glorifies God

No wonder the psalmist said: "It is a good thing to give thanks unto the LORD" (Psalm 92:1). Why? Because when we give thanks based on our faith in the invisible Lord, He is able to lead us out of our restrictions and this gives us a tremendous new perspective. When we give thanks, we notice just how narrow and shortsighted we are.

Sometimes we can't see past our own workload. We can't see past our daily lives. Often our faith is blinded by the trivial. However, if we persevere in prayer, giving thanks to the Lord, God's omnipotence will break through our weakness and defeat the enemy. "Offer unto God thanksgiving...Whoso offereth praise glorifieth me: and to him that ordereth his conversation aright will I shew the salvation of God" (Psalm 50:14, 23). In other words, God's salvation is shown to those who progress from asking and praying to praising and thanksgiving.

Victorious Thanksgiving

How does this personally apply to us? When our prayers are no longer self-centered, but God-centered, He will show us through His Word how we can give thanks for situations such as trials, that by nature, we would not ordinarily be thankful for.

I have often met people who were bitter because somebody had hurt them. As a result, they "closed up." But the Lord wants us to give thanks for all things, according to Ephesians 5:20, "Giving thanks always for all things unto God and the Father in the name of our Lord Jesus Christ."

It has been my own personal experience that I could say with David: "Thou in faithfulness hast afflicted me" (Psalm 119:75). When we have been afflicted and humbled by a family member, neighbor or a friend who has treated us badly, don't retaliate; instead, thank the Lord for such things because James 1:3 says that the testing of our faith produces endurance. Isn't that what we want?

Giving thanks to the Lord allows us to delve deeper into God's nature. In return, the Lord shows us the path of life. If He allows us to be misjudged and humbled, then we must kneel and say: "Thank you for humbling me." David also said: "It is good for me that I have been afflicted..." (Psalm 119:71).

Priestly Thanksgiving

A second reason we should give thanks to the Lord is for the benefit of our Christian brothers and sisters. Many believers waste their time complaining about problems they may have with other believers. This behavior does not glorify God. Instead, we should ask the Lord for boldness and grace to confront those who have wronged us and reconcile the matter in a godly fashion.

Paul, a man of few words who did not exaggerate, said: "I thank my God upon every remembrance of you" (Philippians 1:3). The Philippians were faithful believers who stood by Paul. Of course, one might think that it was easy to give thanks according to the principle, "If you're nice to me I'll be nice to you." It is easy to give thanks for the nice, friendly brethren. But Paul also gave thanks for the difficult and tiresome ones.

The Corinthians had hardly grown in their spiritual lives. Paul had a lot of trouble with them. He had to admonish them, but he also gave thanks for them. With all the strife, quarrelling, envy and backbiting in the Corinthian church, what could Paul possibly have been thankful about? In fact, they even attacked Paul. Yet he prayed: "I thank my God always on your behalf, for the grace of God." The grace of God can be found in even the most difficult of believers.

Unpleasant Thanksgiving

We always have reason to give thanks for our pardon. Herein lies Paul's reason and authority that in spite of everything, he never gave up. Let's not forget, Paul was a man made of flesh and blood. He could have easily said: "I give up...." But he held out until the very end because he always prayed.

To the Church at Thessalonica, he said, "We give thanks to God always for you all, making mention of you in our prayers" (1st Thessalonians 1:2). True intercession is born out of thanksgiving.

Have you been through some unpleasant things recently? The Lord tells us that we are to give thanks not only for the good days, but also for the bad. If we do this, we will penetrate deeper into the nature of God. The Lord will open up one stage of His glory after another and will lead us into His treasury. He reflects the joy of eternity in us because we have become children of God who thank Him for all things, in all situations.

When we do this, we will have entered the process of revival. Revival is so infectious that thousands can be caught up in it through us.

Let's think again of Jehoshaphat: At first he was small, despondent and depressed, no longer knowing what to do. But he broke through in prayer to thanksgiving because he received the Word of God. This was so infectious that all of Jerusalem was able to victoriously resist the enemies in that the inhabitants began to praise and thank the Lord. Shouldn't we do likewise? We have every reason to do so!

Chapter 17

The Restored Altar

"And Elijah said unto all the people, Come near unto
me. And all the people came near unto him. And he
repaired the altar of the LORD that was broken down.
And Elijah took twelve stones, according to the number
of the tribes of the sons of Jacob, unto whom the word
of the LORD came, saying, Israel shall be thy name:
And with the stones he built an altar in the name of the
LORD: and he made a trench about the altar, as great
as would contain two measures of seed"
(1st Kings 18:30–32).

ॐ

The restored altar was the center of divine judgment on Mount Carmel and the beginning of a new revelation of God to Israel. The result was refreshing: Rain poured down upon the dry, parched land.

This shows us that there can never be a new beginning or a new revival before we repair the broken-down altar of the Lord in our hearts and houses.

Notice that Elijah built up the altar of the Lord again when the people stopped crying out to their idols. "And it came to pass, when midday was past, and they prophesied until the time of the offering of the evening sacrifice, that there was neither voice, nor any to answer, nor any that regarded. And Elijah said unto all the people, Come near unto me" (1st Kings 18:29–30a).

The people turned away from Baal and toward God the Lord in that they turned to Elijah. Elijah responded by rebuilding the altar of the Lord that had been broken down.

We all long for a new outpouring of the Holy Spirit, but we need to ask ourselves: When will we be ready to break away from our "idols" of vanity so that we can turn to the Living God with our whole heart?

Why was the altar of the Lord so significant? The word "altar" means "high, exalted place." The altar was the only place where God met with His people, blessing them through the substitutionary sacrifice offered upon it.

Moses' Altar

The Righteous One only meets the sinner in the substitutionary sacrifice of Jesus Christ. This is also how it was at Mount Sinai when the people fled from the voice of God and His holy majesty. Then the Lord said to Moses, "An altar of earth thou shalt make unto me, and shalt sacrifice thereon thy burnt offerings, and thy peace offering, thy sheep, and thine oxen: in all places where I record my name I will come unto thee, and I will bless thee" (Exodus 20:24). So the Lord told Moses that he should build an altar and bring both a burnt offering and a peace offering. God also promised that He would come to him and bless him at this place.

What a wonderful picture of Calvary, where God meets the sinner in the substitutionary sacrifice of the Lord Jesus Christ! Elijah's greatest desire was to bring the backsliders back to the Lord, so it was of primary importance to rebuild the altar of the Lord. If we long for a new contact with the Living God, then we must go to the altar, the only place where the Lord will meet us and bless us. The place of that altar is called Calvary!

Noah's Altar

The altar was always the very first thing men in the Bible set up when they wanted to meet with God. Noah set up the first altar: "And God spake unto Noah, saying, Go forth of the ark, thou, and thy wife, and thy sons, and thy son's wives with thee" (Genesis 8:15–16).

When Noah set foot on the earth that God had judged by sending the flood, we read of this new beginning: "And Noah builded an altar unto the LORD; and took of every clean beast, and of every clean fowl, and offered burnt offerings on the altar" (Genesis 8:20). It is very moving how the Lord, in answer to Noah's action, promised His grace and mercy upon hundreds of generations: "And the LORD smelled a sweet savour; and the LORD said in his heart, I will not again curse the ground any more for man's sake; for the imagination of man's heart is evil from his youth; neither will I again smite any more every thing living, as I have done. While the earth remaineth, seedtime and harvest, and cold and heat, and summer and winter, and day and night shall not cease" (Genesis 18:21–22). It is as though the holy God wants to say, "I will accept the substitutionary sacrifice which is offered for the sins of man." But in the fullness of time, God Himself brought this sacrifice in that He gave His only begotten Son.

Abraham's Altar

Then there was Abraham, who built four altars to the Lord. He built the first one in Sichem after he entered the land of Canaan: "And the LORD appeared unto Abram, and said, Unto thy seed will I give this land; and there builded he an altar unto the LORD, who appeared unto him" (Genesis 12:7). He built the last altar when God commanded him to sacrifice his son Isaac (Genesis 22:9). Throughout the Bible, in the stories of Abraham, Isaac and Jacob, we see many examples of altars built for the Lord.

The altar of burnt offering, which was set up in the forecourt of the Temple, was actually the door to the Holy of Holies. No one could go into the Holy of Holies without first going by the altar of burnt offering.

Finally God Himself, based on His own initiative, set up an altar to sacrifice His very best. He gave Jesus, His only beloved Son, as an eternally valid offering to reconcile lost sinners to Himself. This is what Amos meant when he called to the people in Chapter 4:12: "...prepare to meet thy God, O Israel." In the New Testament we are told, "We have an altar" (Hebrews 13:10). What altar? Calvary! The Cross! The crucified Lord was presented on this altar as a "burnt offering" (a complete offering) so that you and I could have restored fellowship with God.

Having seen the immense significance of the altar as a place of sacrifice, an exalted place and a place of meeting between God and man through the substitutionary sacrifice, we are able to better grasp the meaning of the event on Mount Carmel when the prophet Elijah rebuilt the broken-down altar.

Let's consider the spiritual conditions that lead the eternally faithful God to answer with fire from heaven. In other words, let's ask what we must do so that the fiery power of the Holy Spirit can completely ignite us.

An Altar In The Name Of The Lord

Of Elijah we read: "And with the stones he built an

altar in the name of the LORD: and he made a trench about the altar, as great as would contain two measures of seed. And he put the wood in order, and cut the bullock in pieces, and laid him on the wood..." (1st Kings 18:32–33a). According to 1st Kings 18:31, the altar of the Lord Elijah rebuilt was made with twelve stones: "...according to the number of the tribes of the sons of Jacob, unto whom the word of the LORD came, saying, Israel shall be thy name." Elijah set up a unified Israel by setting up the altar.

This reminds me of 1st Corinthians 10:18, which records an "altar fellowship." The Amplified version of the Bible says: "Consider those physical people of Israel. Are not those who eat the sacrifices partners of the altar — united in their worship of the same God?" Isn't Calvary our altar, and Jesus Christ the One who unites us?

In New Testament terms, the altar of fellowship is the Church of Jesus Christ. To put this into practice is to uphold the true unity of the Church, the obedience in faith. Without an inner unity, there is no fire from above. When two or three are absolutely one in Jesus Christ, they become world conquerors because God sets their hearts on fire with the Holy Spirit. Let's start practicing this organic unity to which we, as regenerate people, belong. We are blood-related! Why do we allow the devil to separate us from our brothers and sisters through mere trifles?

The Restored Altar

Elijah demonstrated what unity among God's people comprises: It is the restored altar! He proclaimed a spiritual law that is valid even today; namely, that unity amongst God's children is the basic condition for the revelation of the Lord's glory! Many of us lead lives that are too individualistic. We are concerned with our own souls and do not bother ourselves with the Church.

A further condition we need to take note of if we are to be filled with the fire of our first love is found in 1st Kings 18:32: "And with the stones he built an altar in the name of the LORD: and he made a trench about the altar, as great as would contain two measures of seed." What was the reason for this unusual act? Let's not answer this hastily. There are several reasons Elijah dug a trench around the altar in the hard, dry earth.

• It served as a border. Elijah made it clear that the people who had drawn near to the altar of fellowship had absolutely nothing to do with the idol worshippers. There must be a separation. If we want God to hear our cries for revival in our soul, then we must make a clear separation today!

• It symbolized depth. It is as though Elijah wanted to say the division must be definite and permanent. At first, those who were standing around did not understand what was taking place. They didn't know that Elijah not only set up the visible altar, but the invisible altar in the heart's of the people.

• It symbolized the trench we need to dig in order to erect the Cross in our hearts. We know of two altars from the Old Testament. The one spoken of in Exodus 27 stood outside in the forecourt in the open air. On this altar, various sacrifices were offered, prophetically pointing to Jesus Christ. But there was also a little altar, the altar of incense. It was hidden in the Holy Place and covered with gold. The incense of prayer arose to the Lord morning and evening.

Elijah's request was for the hearts of the people! In his prayer he cried: "Hear me, O LORD, hear me, that this people may know that thou art the LORD God, and that thou hast turned their heart back again" (1st Kings 18:37). It was quiet at Elijah's inner altar.

Standing next to the light of the Holy Spirit was the Table of Shewbread, the Bread of Life, before the face of God. God doesn't want us to put everything in order and set up our altar again just enough for everything to start rolling. No! The Lord wants more than that; He wants the Cross to be erected in our hearts.

• It had to be filled. "Fill four barrels with water, and pour it on the burnt sacrifice, and on the wood. And he said, Do it the second time. And they did it the second time. And he said, Do it the third time. And they did it the third time. And the water ran round about the altar; and he filled the trench also with water" (verse 33b–35). This trench had to be filled with water, which was hardly to be found at that time. Here an important spiritual law is illuminated: "...not by might, nor by power but by my spirit saith the LORD of hosts" (compare Zechariah 4:6). What a wonderful, clear double significance this precious water in the trench has:

1) It stands for the pure Word of God, which has become rare. We were born again through the washing of water by the Word.

2) This water around the altar precluded any human effort in the prepared sacrifice, which was also drenched in water, making man's fire useless, so that all the glory went to God. Our own fire is easily doused and never consumes our whole being!

How often has a flame sprung up in you, but it turned out only to be emotional enthusiasm. Emotional, "religious" efforts accomplish nothing in terms of eternity. Concerned, believing parents continually urge their children to go to church, Christian camps, or be baptized, but this is all of little use. We cannot ignite the water of the Word with emotional fire. The fire must come from above! We must fulfill the conditions and rebuild the altar in our lives! God will answer with fire from above!

Broken Sacrifice

We see yet another spiritual law revealed in this passage. After the altar was rebuilt and Elijah prepared the wood, it says that he, "...cut the bullock in pieces, and laid him on the wood" (verse 33). We know of five different sacrifices in the Old Testament.

The burnt offering had a special characteristic in that it had to be brought to the Lord whole. Here we are concerned with a burnt offering: "Fill four barrels with water, and pour it on the burnt sacrifice" (verse 33b). It was a whole sacrifice.

We like to speak of complete surrender, but too often we give the Lord nine-tenths and want to keep at least one-tenth for ourselves! We forget that the whole sacrifice was not sacrificed whole, but in pieces. It was a broken sacrifice. This was proof of the authenticity of the burnt offering.

We may speak much of burnt offerings and complete surrender, but a burnt offering accepted by God must be broken. "...he put the wood in order, and cut the bullock in pieces, and laid him on the wood." Nothing is so complete, so whole, as our egos, our personalities. We have a natural desire to assert ourselves. This has utmost priority in our lives under all circumstances.

Do we really want to be aglow with the fire of our first love from above? Then let's thank God for the breaking process in our daily lives! Every wrong that we suffer, and every humiliation we have to bear, is all part of this breaking process.

Evening Sacrifice

The time of this event on Mt. Carmel is very important because it has prophetic meaning: "And it came to pass at the time of the offering of the evening sacrifice, that Elijah the prophet came near, and said,

LORD God of Abraham, Isaac, and of Israel, let it be known this day that thou art God in Israel, and that I am thy servant, and that I have done all these things at thy word. Hear me, O LORD, hear me, that this people may know that thou art the LORD God, and that thou hast turned their heart back again, Then the fire of the LORD fell..." (1st Kings 18:36–38a). It took place at the time of the evening sacrifice: "And it came to pass, when midday was past, and they prophesied until the time of the offering of the evening sacrifice..." (verse 29).

When the time came to bring the evening sacrifice, the sun had set, it began to grow dark, and Elijah started to pray. The fact that this is mentioned twice shows the importance of the timing, because this was the time of the meat offering which was the only offering without blood. It was made of fine flour, oil and frankincense, and pointed to the holy, immaculate life of the Lord Jesus.

When it was time for the realization of Israel's sanctification, the whole sacrifice was brought and the altar set up again. Here the meat offering and the burnt offering coincide; true sanctification is also complete surrender. When? In the evening.

Your Decision

With great earnestness we see that it is already evening now. "The night cometh when no man can work!"

Here it was late in Israel's history and judgment

was imminent, but once again the altar was set up and once again the Lord revealed Himself in a wonderful way.

He wanted so much to reveal Himself to His people because He loved them. He said through the prophet Jeremiah: "With loving-kindness have I drawn thee." Do you notice that the night of the endtimes has descended upon us? Will you repair the broken-down altar in your life, your family, and your heart? The night is drawing near. God the Lord is ready to consume all that which is no good in your heart with His holy fire. You have the Word of God, the water, but it has to be ignited by the fire from above. Are you willing for this to take place? Or will you miss this last chance?

It is time for you to take holiness seriously. The Scriptures warn us to strive after "...holiness, without which no man shall see the LORD." Surrender yourself completely. The meat offering and burnt offering will coincide. Don't wait any longer; do not halt between two opinions, for: "Yet a little while, and he that shall come will come, and will not tarry." The Lord Jesus, our meat and burnt offering, is coming soon! The spiritual constellation is very clear; the meat and burnt offering take place together. The holiness and glory of Jesus Christ will soon be revealed to His saints. Set up your altar again before it is too late.

Maranatha, come quickly, Lord Jesus!

Chapter 18

Three Stages of Revival

"And Elijah the Tishbite, who was of the inhabitants
of Gilead, said unto Ahab, as the LORD God of Israel
liveth, before whom I stand, there shall not be dew nor
rain these years, but according to my word"
(1st Kings 17:1).

⁂

After Elijah spoke these words to Ahab, three
years of drought began, but during this
period of drought (in New Testament
language we could say "in this time a spiritual
drought is a lack of revival"), we are shown three

stages of revival:
1. The way to personal revival
2. Revival that spreads to others
3. Breakthrough to general revival

Personal Revival

After Elijah delivered his message, "There shall not be dew nor rain these years, but according to my word," God gave him a new task. While divine judgment in the form of a spiritual drought came upon the people, Elijah was in the midst of revival: "And the word of the LORD came unto him, saying, Get thee hence, and turn thee eastward, and HIDE thyself by the brook of Cherith, that is before Jordan" (verses 2–3). Only hiding made it possible in the midst of spiritual drought to have revival and to remain revived.

Therefore, hide yourself, just as the Lord Jesus hid Himself in the midst of great rejection: "But Jesus hid himself, and went out of the temple" (John 8:59).

Jesus disappeared in that He surrendered His life. This resulted in a worldwide, eternally valid revival. "Hide yourself!" By not wanting to make an appearance, you surrender your self-assertion and the Lord's blessing of revival begins.

For Elijah, water was the lifeline: "...thou shalt drink of the brook" (verse 4). Just imagine: A parching drought had come upon the land. Both man and beast suffered unspeakably from thirst. In the midst of this drought, Elijah found the brook of which God spoke to him.

Why did this happen to Elijah, of all people? Because he had no other support than the Word of the Lord. Such people have this promise: "Blessed is the man that trusteth in the LORD, and whose hope the LORD is. For he shall be as a tree planted by the waters, and that spreadeth out her roots by the river, and shall not be careful in the year of drought, neither shall cease from yielding fruit" (Jeremiah 17:7–8). Let nobody say that revival isn't for our day. Whoever has his roots on the river, whoever drinks from the river of life, whoever has living fellowship with the Lord is a revived person in the midst of a spiritual drought.

The Lord's second command to Elijah went a step further: "...I have commanded the ravens to feed thee there" (1st Kings 17:4). Ravens were considered unclean birds. Elijah, zealous for the Law of God, now had to receive his food from the ravens. What a humiliation! But herein is the secret, for it is written: "For thus saith the high and lofty One that inhabiteth eternity, whose name is Holy; I dwell in the high and holy place, with him also that is of the contrite and humble spirit, to revive the spirit of the humble, and to revive the heart of the contrite ones" (Isaiah 57:15). Elijah, a mighty man of God, had to hide himself. But in hiding, the well of life opened up to him. As he drank of it, he was deeply humbled. He identified himself with those unclean ravens.

First Kings 17:5 says: "So he went and did according unto the word of the LORD," and therefore he was quickened. Elijah was a man of revival who was surrounded by a lack of revival. This is a message for our time. When you are willing to disappear in the death of the Lord, springs of living waters will open up to you. You will be humbled, but at the same time, you will receive divine nourishment.

Spreading Of Revival

Then comes the second stage of revival; namely, its spreading to like-minded people. What sort of people are they? They are also people who have nothing. In Elijah's case, it was the Gentile widow. Here again, Elijah acted upon the Word of the Lord alone. When he had passed the first test, a new task was given to him: "And the word of the LORD came unto him, saying, Arise, get thee to Zarephath, which belongeth to Zidon, and dwell there: behold, I have commanded a widow woman there to substain thee" (1st Kings 17:8–9). Therefore, on the grounds of the Word of the Lord, it is possible to pass on the blessing we have received to others. God never demands anything of us which is impossible in practice. The Lord Jesus said, "He that believeth on me, as the scripture hath said, out of his belly shall flow rivers of living water." This is also possible in the midst of a spiritual drought. It is even so that when the practical fulfillment of God's promises have become impossible in our eyes, God has already begun to fulfill them.

What kind of woman was Elijah to go to? Not only

was she a Gentile widow, but she was impoverished as well. She confessed, "...I have nothing." Whenever we become empty of ourselves and are convinced that we can do nothing and we have nothing, the fullness of God breaks through, providing obedience and faith.

In 1st Kings 17:14, Elijah said these words on behalf of the Lord: "For thus saith the LORD God of Israel, The barrel of meal shall not waste, neither shall the cruse of oil fail, until the day that the LORD sendeth rain upon the earth." That is revival in the midst of a spiritual drought. A revived Elijah passed on revival to this poor Gentile widow. Thus, after personal revival, revival also spreads to others.

General Revival

This general revival consisted of the prayer of the repentance of a single revived person. It says of Elijah, "...and he cast himself down upon the earth, and put his face between his knees" (1st Kings 18:42). This means that he humbled himself before the Lord. The outcome of this repentance can be found in 1st Kings 18:45: "And it came to pass in the mean while, that the heaven was black with clouds and wind, and there was a great rain." The blessing of personal revival became available to all of Israel!

Our hearts long for the Lord to grant us this great rain in our day also. He will do it when we allow ourselves to be revived, when our lives become a blessing to our surroundings and when we humble ourselves more deeply, even for the sins of others. Then the Lord will send a mighty general revival according to His unchanging promise.

Chapter 19

Revival Among God's People

"And Hezekiah rejoiced, and all the people, that God had prepared the people: for the thing was done suddenly" (2nd Chronicles 29:36).

୨●

Revival is necessary so that believers burn again and become full of the Holy Spirit. Revival among God's people brings about a solution to many questions and problems. Revival would mean that the challenge of evangelizing the world would be solved in one moment because every single one of God's people would start to evangelize. The questions of unity and victory in our everyday lives would be answered by revival in our hearts!

Where Does Revival Begin?

Revival among God's people begins with the individual. In 2nd Chronicles 29, it began with the 25-year-old King Hezekiah. This man had a burden for revival and a vision for the plight of God's people. Where did he get this burden? "And he did that which was right in the sight of the LORD, according to all that David his father had done" (2nd Chronicles 29:2). He was obedient to the Lord in practice. Let's look at the seven-fold obedience of Hezekiah:

1) He Was Obedient To The Lord

The Bible says of him: "He did that which was right in the sight of the LORD." Are we doing likewise?

2) He Had An Open Sanctuary

"He...opened the doors of the house of the LORD" (verse 3). Hezekiah acted immediately, not after he had been reigning for a long time but, "...in the FIRST year of his reign, in the FIRST month." Brothers and sisters, our bodies are a sanctuary that should be a temple of the Holy Spirit. Is this sanctuary open to the Lord? Can He enter?

3) He Repaired The Doors

"He...opened the doors of the house of the LORD, and repaired them" (verse 3). Not only did He open the doors in an act of obedience, but he repaired them as well. This is an expression of continuous obedience. An emotional "yes" to the Lord, which is quickly turned into a "no" in our daily lives, is ultimately worthless. If we are obedient in church by singing, praying, listening and saying "Amen" to what's taught, then we go home and close the door so that it becomes unholy in and around us, we belong to those who say "Lord, Lord," but do not the will of the Father, as the Lord Jesus said in Matthew 7:21.

That is why the third aspect of Hezekiah's obedience is so important. He repaired the doors he had opened. Our Lord Jesus also testified of Himself, "...the Father has not left me alone; for I do ALWAYS those things that please Him" (John 8:29). That is continuous obedience.

4) He Re-enlisted The Priests And Levites

"And he brought in the priests and the Levites, and gathered them together..." (verse 4). The priests and Levites had forgotten their high calling. Notice the words, "...he brought in"! In other words, he placed them in another position. Hezekiah's revived condition was the cause. The effect was that all the priests and Levites were gathered and brought into the sanctuary. What a glorious message! When the doors of my sanctuary, my heart, are open wide to the Lord, I have authority to bring other priests, other believers, into a new position.

5) He Gathered Them

"He...gathered them together into the east street" (verse 4:b). Hezekiah gathered the priests and the Levites and showed them new perspectives. At the same time, he led them to a renewal to the Lord. This is what a person with a burden for revival does. Do you have this burden? Does it weigh heavily upon you? Let's take one another by the hand and gather together in the street on the east; that is to say, let's look unto Jesus, the author of our faith, and lay aside every weight and sin.

6) He Revealed The Damage

Hezekiah revealed the damage through the preaching of the Word. He told them the cause of their lack of revival, "For our fathers have trespassed, and done that which was evil in the eyes of the LORD our God...Wherefore the wrath of the LORD was upon Judah and Jerusalem" (verse 6 and 8). In verse 5, he called upon them to sanctify themselves: "Hear me, ye Levites, sanctify now yourselves, and sanctify the house of the LORD God of your fathers." Not only did he bring them into the sanctuary, but he revealed their sins unsparingly.

7) He Renewed The Covenant With The Lord

"Now it is in mine heart to make a covenant with the LORD God of Israel, that his fierce wrath may turn away from us" (verse 10). Is this necessary today? Absolutely. Many have desecrated the New Covenant of the blood of Jesus Christ. That is the reason for all the lukewarmness and spiritual sluggishness.

We can summarize the seven-fold obedience of King Hezekiah with one word: Action! He did that which was right in the sight of the Lord! What has the Lord told you to do? Stop crying, lamenting and weeping and act now in the Name of Jesus. Do what the Holy Spirit is telling you to do! Thus saith the Lord: "Why call ye me, Lord, Lord, and do not the things which I say?" (Luke 6:46). And in James 1:22 we read, "Be ye doers of the word, and not hearers only, deceiving your own selves." What must you do then? Exactly what the Lord is telling you to do: "This is the will of God, even your sanctification!" Hezekiah did that which was right in the sight of the Lord.

After the young King Hezekiah gathered the priests and Levites in the street on the east, he revealed six sins to them. These are also six hidden sins of believers today:

1. They Trespassed

The first sin Hezekiah named in verse 6 was, "For our fathers have trespassed, and done that which was evil in the eyes of the LORD our God, and have forsaken him." Outwardly they remained God's people, but inwardly they were seduced by idols: "...and have forsaken him." They worshipped images alongside their usual worship of God.

Isn't this the sin of many believers today? Outwardly, they appear to be believers, but in their hearts they have forsaken Him. I can almost hear the prophet Azariah saying to Asa: "The LORD is with you, while ye be with him; and if ye seek him, he will be found of you; but if ye forsake him he will forsake you" (2nd Chronicles 15:2). If your heart is filled with something other than His glory, then you have forsaken Him. Perhaps you may have felt for a long time that He was grieved and His Spirit had to withdraw.

2. They Turned Their Backs

The second sin Hezekiah named is found in verse 6b: "...and have turned away their faces from the habitation of the LORD, and turned their backs." They were looking in another direction. They turned their backs on the sanctuary where God's presence was.

With sorrow in my heart I have seen believers who used to burn for the Lord turn their backs on the sanctuary. They made no change for the better. When your faith no longer grows because you have turned your back on the sanctuary and when you are no longer convicted, cleansed and sanctified all the time, then everything dwindles away to nothing in your spiritual life and you become like the man in James 1:23–24: "...beholding his natural face in a glass: For he beholdeth himself, and goeth his way, and

straightway forgetteth what manner of man he was."
The person who turns his back on the mirror of the
Word of God represents the majority of today's
superficial believers. They hear the Word of God and
are somewhat moved by it, but as soon as the
"Amen" has been said, they turn their backs on God's
demand on their lives. They return to their daily rou-
tines and forget what manner of men they are.

3. They Shut The Doors

The third sin Hezekiah revealed is found in 2nd
Chronicles 29:7: "Also they have shut up the doors of
the porch." The worship services ceased and the
doors were closed. Why? Because of convenience. It
became dark in the Temple and the priests no longer
went in and out.

When we turn to 1st Corinthians 6:19, we read
that our bodies are temples of the Holy Spirit and are
not our own because we were bought with a price.
This helps us understand with shocking clarity what
the Holy Spirit says to us: "Also they have shut up the
doors of the porch!" That this is especially mentioned
shows how very much it grieves the Lord. The doors
to His sanctuary were closed.

I am compelled to say very loudly and forcefully
that we are surrounded today by believers who, in
their lives of haste and in their pursuit of material
things and the satisfaction of sensual lusts, have
closed the doors of their hearts to the Lord. In their
lives, as with the priests and Levites, everything has

become a farce and a mockery. Outwardly, they were priests and Levites, but the true life, the essence, the surrender of their hearts, was missing.

Today it is a fact that many who call themselves "Christians," in reality have closed their hearts to the Lord Jesus. When I put my ear to the Bible, I hear the Lord weeping over the distant hearts of His children as He says, "This people draweth nigh unto me with their mouth, and honoureth me with their lips; but their heart is far from me" (Matthew 15:8). Oh, if only I could take hold of you, Christians without Christ, shake you and cry, "Wake up, you that have a name that you live and are dead!"

4. The Light Went Out

The fourth sin Hezekiah mentioned is also recorded in verse 7, "...and put out the lamps." The Lord commanded Moses that the lamps on the golden candlestick were to burn continuously. The priests went in regularly to check them; the wicks were cleaned and the oil was replenished. This was the only light in the sanctuary, for there was no window. It was pitch black when the doors to the sanctuary were closed. When anyone went in, he bumped into the candlestick. Thus the candlestick became a curse instead of a blessing. There was no natural light in the sanctuary; there was only the oil-fed lights of the lamps.

Today we face the terrible fact that it has become spiritually dark in many churches. There is light —

the light of the intellect, culture and some theology —
but what is lacking is the light of the lamp, which is
fed by the oil of the Holy Spirit. The light from above
convicts, penetrates and reveals our heart. How
urgently Jesus said, "Ye are the light of the world"
(Matthew 5:14) and "Let your light so shine before
men" (Matthew 5:16).

Again, let's ask ourselves, what kind of light is
that? The answer is found in Revelation 21:23: "And
the city had no need of the sun, neither of the moon,
to shine in it: for the glory of God did lighten it, and
the Lamb is the light thereof." That type of light
describes only those who follow the Lamb, who are
with the Lamb and do what is right in the sight of the
Lord. In spite of our religious activity it has become
dark in many of our churches, our families and even
our lives because we have put out the lamps!

5. No Incense Offered

We find the fifth sin that Hezekiah brought to light
in 2nd Chronicles 29:7, "...and have not burned
incense." Here I have to speak about the great mys-
tery of prayer again. The incense was offered on the
golden altar which stood in the sanctuary, immediately in front of the veil which led into the Holy of
Holies, into the presence of God. This incense is a
wonderful picture of the prayers of believers. This is
explained twice in the book of Revelation: "And
when he had taken the book, the four beasts and four
and twenty elders fell down before the Lamb, having

every one of them harps, and golden vials full of odours, which are the prayers of the saints...And another angel came and stood at the altar, having a golden censer; and there was given unto him much incense, that he should offer it with the prayers of all saints upon the golden altar which was before the throne. And the smoke of the incense, which came with the prayers of the saints, ascended up before God out of the angel's hand" (Revelation 5:8, 8:3–4).

The mighty effect the prayers of the saints have can be seen from Revelation 8:5: "And the angel took the censer, and filled it with fire of the altar, and cast it into the earth: and there were voices, and thunderings, and lightnings, and an earthquake." The power of prayer is portrayed here. But simultaneously, through Hezekiah's mouth, we are shown the terrible sin of omission of believers, "...and have not burned incense" (2nd Chronicles 29:7).

The exalted Lord said to the Church in Ephesus, "Nevertheless I have somewhat against thee, because thou hast left they first love. Remember therefore from whence thou art fallen, and repent, and do the first works; or else I will come unto thee quickly, and will remove thy candlestick out of his place, except thou repent" (Revelation 2:4–5). Here we have it! If repentance was not lacking, a revival would begin. The closed doors of our hearts, the extinguished lamps and the lacking incense are an expression of our unrepentance. Where are the people who pray today? We have no idea of what the Lord can and will do if we pray.

The Lord Jesus said: "Ask, and it shall be given you; seek, and ye shall find; knock, and it shall be opened unto you" (Matthew 7:7). Have your prayer wings become weary? Are your prayers made hastily and therefore ineffective? If only you knew what prayer from a cleansed heart could do!

6. No Burnt Offerings

The sixth sin Hezekiah named at the end of verse 7 was, "...nor offered burnt offerings in the holy place unto the God of Israel." We know that in contrast to the other offerings, the burnt offering was a whole offering, an expression of the complete dedication of the one bringing it. Everything had to be sacrificed to the Lord; nothing was to be withheld.

It is significant that Hezekiah mentioned the burnt offering, guilt offering, thank offering and wave offering. Why? Because the Lord only wants complete dedication. Half-heartedness is an abomination to Him.

These six sins believers commit reveal their lack of revival.

Chapter 20

The Last Preparation For Revival

"Wherefore the wrath of the LORD was upon Judah
and Jerusalem, and he hath delivered them to trouble, to
astonishment, and to hissing, as ye see with your eyes.
For, lo, our fathers have fallen by the sword, and our
sons and our daughters and our wives are in
captivity for this"
(2nd Chronicles 29:8–9).

۳۰

H ezekiah showed the people the result of their
condition. They are the same four results we
see today:

1. "Wherefore the wrath of the LORD was upon Judah and Jerusalem..." (verse 8). Persistent disobedience, lukewarmness and indifference arouse God's wrath. Even though Scripture says that He is slow to anger, we see today with great fear and trembling how God's wrath is coming upon the Christian church, which is seen by the fact that His hand of blessing is being withdrawn.

2. "...and he hath delivered them to trouble, to astonishment..." (verse 8). The lack of revival caused trouble and dispersion. Further commentary on our times is unnecessary. Despite all attempts to produce unity — which are a complete failure because the Church of Jesus Christ cannot be organized — believers are more dispersed, and in more trouble, than ever before.

3. "...and to hissing, as ye see with your eyes..." (verse 8). This is the shame we suffer, and not because we are disciples of Jesus but because the world says of the believers: "Your deeds speak so loudly that we cannot hear your words." The world despises God's people.

4. "For, lo, our fathers have fallen by the sword, and our sons and our daughters and our wives are in captivity for this" (verse 9). The fourth result speaks of war and danger. A spiritual judgment is upon the Church of Jesus Christ and a terrible judgment of war threatens the world. What is the cause? A lack of revival among God's people. The world is crying out for political solutions, but it finds none because there is only a spiritual

solution: Revival among God's people.

Therefore, will you humble yourself today and open the door of your heart so that it becomes light again, incense can be burned and you are completely dedicated to the Lord? Then a revival will spread through your life to your surroundings.

Let's ask again: What is the reason for the above-mentioned negative results? Terrible things happened because of the sins of the believers. We see this from Hezekiah's urgent appeal in verse 5b, "...carry forth the filthiness out of the holy place." He revealed the deepest need of God's people. He is saying, "Garbage and dirt have piled up in the Holy of Holies because you have closed the doors, extinguished the lamps and offered no incense." Because you have closed the doors to the Lord and He can no longer come in, sin and garbage have collected in the heart of your temple. The results are often depression, powerlessness, resignation and even doubt concerning the reality of one's redemption. Heed the call to, "...carry forth the filthiness out of the holy place."

The Great Challenge

After God convicted the people of their sins, Hezekiah showed them the way to revival. He felt that the priests and Levites were coming to a dangerous vacuum and the question was decisive: Would they obey the Word of the Lord or not? You, too, can hear the call to be sanctified.

Hezekiah must have noticed this danger, for he suddenly called, "My sons, be not now negligent: for the LORD hath chose you to stand before him, to serve him, and that ye should minister unto him, and burn incense" (verse 11). Jesus Christ said, "I have chosen you, and ordained you, that ye should go and bring forth fruit" (John 15:16). Are you a child of God? If you answer "yes," then God has chosen you; He has predestined you to be a vessel of revival. In spirit, I feel that we have reached a dangerous point. Will you respond to God's demands?

The Beginning Of Revival

When we follow the story in 2nd Chronicles 29, we can thankfully say that they responded. "Then the Levites arose..." (verse 12). Then a whole list of names is mentioned. We see how seriously God takes this. He knows by name those who are willing to respond to His Word in faithful obedience. However, the point mentioned at the end of verse 34 puts us to shame: "...for the Levites were more upright in heart to sanctify themselves than the priests." The Levites were inferior as far as their office was concerned, and they also did the menial work. The priests belonged to the upper class, the religious leaders, but they were less zealous to be sanctified. Then, as now, the Word of the Lord applied: "...the last shall be first" (Matthew 19:30).

Revival will begin when we do that which the Levites and priests did: "...they gathered their brethren, and sanctified themselves, and came, according to the commandment of the king, by the words of the LORD, to cleanse the house of the LORD" (verse 15).

Revival did not break out immediately, but only after the priests and Levites took certain steps toward it. It is no use to pray for revival if we are not willing to fulfill the conditions. The condition is a thorough cleansing of our sanctuary. "Now they began on the first day of the month to sanctify, and on the eighth day of the month came they to the porch of the LORD: so they sanctified the house of the LORD in eight days" (verse 17). They were busy cleansing and sanctifying themselves and the sanctuary for sixteen days.

I am absolutely convinced that the Lord wants to begin this revival in our hearts right now if we allow ourselves to be cleansed. Read 2nd Chronicles 29:16. A significant word is written there: "And the priests went into the inner part of the house..." They went into the inner part of the house of the Lord to cleanse and remove all the impurity found in the Temple. The Levites received it and carried it out to the Brook of Kidron. Then they reopened the sanctuary doors, let the bright sunshine stream in to reveal all the filth, and began the work.

In the same way, Jesus Christ, our heavenly High Priest, wants you to become willing at this very moment to open the door of your sanctuary. He is standing before the door of your heart and waiting, for He still says today: "Behold, I stand at the door, and knock..." (Revelation 3:20). If you open the door, He will come in. He will reveal the deepest need of your heart, illuminate the most hidden corners and bring to light all of your accumulated sin: pride, arrogance, impurity, greed, irreconcilability and dogmatic nature. I often fear that much preaching goes in one ear and out the other. This message will be in vain if you do not allow Jesus Christ to penetrate your heart. Whoever allows the Lord to do this will be revived, and through him, others.

The Sacrificial Lamb

How did the revival of Hezekiah's time break out? The first sign of revival was that the slain Lamb became the central point of all Israel again: "And they brought seven bullocks, and seven rams, and seven lambs, and seven he goats, for a sin offering for the kingdom, and for the sanctuary, and for Judah. And he commanded the priests the sons of Aaron to offer them on the altar of the LORD. So they killed the bullocks, and the priests received the blood, and sprinkled it on the altar: likewise, when they had killed the rams, they sprinkled the blood upon the altar: they killed also the lambs, and they sprinkled the blood upon the altar. And the priests killed them, and they made reconciliation with their blood upon the altar, to make an atonement for all Israel: for the king commanded that the burnt offering and the sin offering should be made for all Israel" (verses 21–22,

24). The first mighty sign of revival is that Jesus the Lamb is exalted in our midst. Then the whole congregation can begin to worship.

The second sign of revival was: "And all the congregation worshipped..." (verse 28). We read that the king also bowed his head. He, and all those who were present with him, worshipped (verse 30).

The third sign of revival was that great joy broke out among the people. The Lord speedily granted the revival: "And Hezekiah rejoiced, and all the people, that God has prepared the people: for the thing was done suddenly" (verse 36).

Chapter 21

A Solemn Call for Revival

"Keep silence before me, O islands; and let the people
renew their strength: let them come near; then let them
speak: let us come near together to judgment"
(Isaiah 41:1).

❦

This call for revival is directed especially to
Gentiles. The nations are requested to be silent in
connection with His dealings in regard to Israel.

Isaiah 41:5–7 describes the Gentiles' vain idolatry.
Then in verse 8, we read, "But thou, Israel, art my
servant, Jacob whom I have chosen, the seed of

Abraham my friend."

The words of Isaiah 41:1 apply to us because if they apply to Gentiles, then they also apply to Gentile Christians. "Keep silence before me, O islands."

There is clearly a controversy between the eternal God and the Gentiles, and He tells them to be silent. You, too, should stop contradicting Him! He, the highest, the eternal and holy God, whom we worship and honor, commands us to be silent, for what He is revealing today through the "worm Jacob" should have become visible long ago in a spiritual sense in the Church of Jesus Christ. He commands us to be silent with our dogma, for we may have the doctrine, but our lives are lacking evidence thereof.

The Lord wants us to be still before Him and be strengthened, "...let the people renew their strength." After this, we are to draw near to Him and finally speak with Him in holy boldness. We have heard how in the past He has poured out His Holy Spirit, and we know of mighty revivals. We hear the moving sound of the Spirit of God in Israel — God is working with His nation again. May the Holy Spirit convict us today and may the solemn call for revival burn deeply within our hearts!

1. Keep Silent!

Psalm 46:10 says, "Be still, and know that I am God." He is the One before whom the universe trembles. He is the Lord for whom a thousand years is as one day. He is the Almighty One, for He rules the world! However, I must add at this point that whatever we may say to Him in holiness and faith must never be hasty or come with flippant familiarity, because although He is our Father, He is our Father in heaven and we are on earth! He is our Friend, but at the same time He is also our Judge. He is merciful, but He is also holy and righteous! That is why He said, "Keep silence before me, O islands."

Let us first be silent, ashamed and convicted that Isaiah 41:15 is not a reality in our lives. We can see this fact today in Israel: "Behold, I will make thee a new sharp threshing instrument having teeth: thou shalt thresh the mountains, and beat them small, and shalt make the hills as chaff." We cannot use our weakness as an excuse because Israel is described in the previous verse as being small and weak: "Fear not, thou worm Jacob" (verse 14). It is through Israel's weakness and helplessness that the Lord reveals His power!

Are You Ready For Revival?

Why is there no revival? Why is there a conflict between God and our souls? Amos 3:3 reads, "Can two walk together, except they be agreed?" Be silent before Him, because if you have departed even slightly from Him, He has also departed from you. This is written in 2nd Chronicles 15:2: "The LORD is with you, while ye be with him; and if ye seek him, he will be found of you; but if ye forsake him, He will forsake you."

We have every reason to be silent before God! He has certainly blessed us up to the present day. He has given us so much in spite of our unfaithfulness and failures. Be silent before Him and consider His grace.

We are living in a century populated by foolish Christians in whom there is no continual spirit of prayer, no breakthrough in faith. That is why we don't have a continuing revival. But God wants revival and He is solemnly calling us today.

The question is: Are you ready for revival? Should the Lord give a mighty moving of His Holy Spirit in our days? Are you ready to receive and care for the many babes in Christ who will be born, greet them warmly instead of passing them by as if you could care less? Are you praying for God's grace? Are you making use of the grace you have already received, or was it until this day, in vain? You want more power, but what about the power of Christ who indwells you? Consider these questions earnestly and be still!

Think about what the Lord could do through you and what He has not been able to do because of your disobedience. When you think this over, you will see that God is ready and willing to do what is written in Ephesians 3:20: "Now unto him that is able to do exceeding abundantly above all that we ask or think, according to the power that worketh in us."

We can divide this verse into four parts:

1) He is able;
2) He can do all;
3) He can do above all; and

4) He can do exceeding abundantly above all.

That is the power that works in us through Jesus Christ! What about this power? Why is there still no breakthrough? Do you understand now why the Lord calls you to be silent before Him? Do you really want to receive what you are praying for?

Many people speak and sing about Jesus with adoration, but they sing, pray and preach without considering the condition of their own proud hearts. Be silent before Him! You cannot expect Him to ever answer if you are not willing to hear Him. Be silent before Him because God wants to speak to you today!

The psalmist said, "I will hear what God the LORD will speak..." (Psalm 85:8). It is important to be silent before Him now, because when you hear His voice in your heart, you will find that there is no voice like His. His Word sweeps out all of your hidden pride, selfishness and untruthfulness in order for Jesus to come in and be glorified. He wants to speak to you now in such a way that His Word can work spirit and life into you. Be silent in your innermost being also, in that you submit yourself to Him unreservedly.

You need the Holy Spirit because you are to be a legible epistle of Jesus Christ that bears His seal. In olden days, the wax for sealing a letter had to be soft so that the seal could be impressed upon it. Many Christians are hard, not soft. What does God want to do in your life? He wants Jesus to be formed in you!

Be silent as long as Galatians 4:19 and Romans 8:29 have not been realized in your life. Paul called to the Galatians: "My little children, of whom I travail in birth again until Christ be formed in you." When you recognize yourself and humble yourself, then you can take the next step described in our text.

2. Renew Your Strength!

"Keep silence before me, O islands; and let the people renew their strength..." (Isaiah 41:1). You will receive new strength from God and new power through the Holy Spirit when you kneel at His feet in silence and humble yourself. When the whole truth about you is brought to light and your wretchedness is revealed, acknowledge it and He will renew your strength.

How can your strength be renewed? Acknowledge that you have spoken many religious words, but the power of the Holy Spirit, the power of Him before whom you are now silent, was lacking.

There are people who have a terrific urge to speak; they talk and talk, but it is only like chaff because they have nothing to say. Be silent and let Jesus speak! Let His wounds speak to you, for they are reality. May His death and His resurrection move your heart. Let the trumpet call proclaiming His return, which we hear, shatter your soul. These are all realities, just as real as the Lord wants to renew your strength. The eternal Spirit is with you, but you miss His power because you lend your ear to all sorts of voices except His.

Even our own voices harm us because they are often heard without our having had a meeting with the Lord. This is why the Bible says: "For if the trumpet give an uncertain sound, who shall prepare himself to the battle?" (1st Corinthians 14:8). Have you noticed that your testimony has no power and that you are using your own words when your strength has not been renewed? This is all the result of your not being silent before Him.

The Waters Of Blessings

What can we tell people of Him if He has not been able to speak to us? Be silent before Him, and let Him renew your strength. Then the blessed Spirit of the Lord will cause our cold hearts to glow and He will shake us out of our fatal lethargy. He wants to renew your spiritual strength in such a way that in the days to come there will be streams of living water flowing from every one of us. What a stream of blessing will flow in your family and your church! People will swim in this stream of living water with you!

Ezekiel may have had little or no inclination to swim as he waded in this river of life, which first reached his ankles, then his knees, then his loins. Finally it became so deep that the had to admit, "...the waters were risen, waters to swim in, a river that could not be passed over" (Ezekiel 47:5). This is the compulsion from above which sinners cannot resist. They HAVE to throw themselves into the river of salvation.

May the power of the Holy Spirit so come upon us and stream through us that multitudes of sinners have to be converted.

Our Lord Jesus promised, "He that believeth on me, as the scripture hath said, out of his belly shall flow rivers of living water" (John 7:38). How does this happen? Be silent before Him and let your strength be renewed in that you remind Him of this promise.

This is the wonderful part: When we humbly recognize and confess our sins, the power of God, the power of faith, comes over us and we are able to remind Him of His promises: "For I will pour water upon him that is thirsty, and floods upon the dry ground: I will pour my spirit upon thy seed, and my blessing upon thine offspring" (Isaiah 44:3): This means your family, church, and you personally.

You can also renew your strength in that you surrender your own strength and wisdom. I can testify to you that I am never so filled with the Holy Spirit as when I am empty of myself. I am never as strong as I am in extreme weakness. The cause of our sinful weakness is our own strength. The cause of our sinful foolishness is our natural human wisdom. We can only pray, "Lord, help us now to be silent before You and receive new strength." Then are we able to come near.

3. Come Near!

"Keep silence before me, O islands; and let the people renew their strength: let them come near together to judgment."

You are invited to draw near when you have humbled yourself, when you have been silent and your strength has been renewed. Draw near now as Abraham did when He heard what the Lord intended to do to Sodom and Gomorrah, "And Abraham drew near..." (Genesis 18:23). As a believer, you must realize how close you already are to Him! "But now in Christ Jesus ye who sometimes were far off are made nigh by the blood of Christ" (Ephesians 2:13). We are hidden with Christ in God. Now you can draw near in faith. But consider to whom you are coming: your Father. What a precious Word of the Lord that the Father Himself loves us! Remember when you draw near to Him, He also wants to draw near to you. What you feel, He also feels. We wrestle and pray for many souls to break through to a living faith in Jesus. Remember, we not only have the King's ear but also the King's heart! Base your claim upon His Word and He will hear you.

4. Now Speak!

"Let them come near; then let them speak." Then you may say in adoring thankfulness and in humble freedom, "Lord it is time for you to act. What would the enemy say if we were to be defeated now? Your Name must be glorified." If you have truly surrendered your whole being to Him, you may speak boldly. I implore you not to lie to Him and say, "Here is my all, Lord" if you are not really giving it to Him. Give everything to the Lord so that you belong to Him completely. This is the solemn call of God to revival, and it is addressed to you!

➡ *Tap into the Bible analysis of top prophecy authorities...*

Midnight Call is a hard-hitting Bible-based magazine loaded with news, commentary, special features, and teaching, illustrated with explosive color pictures and graphics. Join hundreds of thousands of readers in 140 countries who enjoy this magazine regularly!

➤ *The world's leading prophetic Bible magazine*

➤ *Covering international topics with detailed commentary*

➤ *Bold, uncompromising Biblical stands on issues*

➤ *Pro-Bible, Pro-family, Pro-life*

12 issues/1 yr. $28.95
24 issues/2 yr. $45